Leaving Leningrad

BRANDEIS SERIES ON JEWISH WOMEN

Shulamit Reinharz, General Editor
Joyce Antler, Associate Editor
Sylvia Barack Fishman, Associate Editor
Susan Kahn, Associate Editor

The Hadassah Research Institute on Jewish Women, established at Brandeis University in 1997 by Hadassah, the Women's Zionist Organization of America, Inc., supports interdisciplinary basic and applied research as well as cultural projects on Jewish women around the world. Under the auspices of the Institute, the Brandeis Series on Jewish Women publishes a wide range of books by and about Jewish women in diverse contexts and time periods.

Marjorie Agosín, *Uncertain Travelers: Conversations with Jewish Women Immigrants to America,* 1999

Rahel R. Wasserfall, *Women and Water: Menstruation in Jewish Life and Law,* 1999

Susan Starr Sered, *What Makes Women Sick: Militarism, Maternity, and Modesty in Israeli Society,* 2000

Pamela S. Nadell and Jonathan D. Sarna, *Women and American Judaism: Historical Perspectives,* 2001

Ludmila Shtern, *Leaving Leningrad,* 2001

Leaving Leningrad

Ludmila Shtern

Brandeis University Press

Published by University Press of New England

Hanover and London

Brandeis University Press

Published by University Press of New England, Hanover, NH 03755

© 2001 by Brandeis University Press

Printed in the United States of America

5 4 3 2 1

Library of Congress Cataloging-in-Publication Data

Shtern, Ludmila.
    Leaving Leningrad / Ludmila Shtern.
        p. cm. — (Brandeis series on Jewish women)
    ISBN 1-58465-100-8 (alk. paper)
    1. Shtern, Ludmila. 2. Jews — Russia — Saint Petersburg — Biography.
    3. Saint Petersburg (Russia) — Biography. 4. Jews,
Russian — Massachusetts — Boston — Biography. 5. Jewish
women — Massachusetts — Boston — Biography. 6. Boston (Mass.) — Biography.
I. Title. II. Series.
    DS135.R95 S5378 2001
        947'.21004924'0092 — dc21   2001001473

To my mother and father

Contents

Acknowledgments

I would like to acknowledge several people without whom the English translation of this book would have never materialized.

First of all, my deep gratitude goes to Rachael Morgenstern for her hard and heroic work in translating my book despite its vernacular Russian.

I am grateful to my bilingual friend Rima Zolina for editing and polishing the English text and for making this translation as authentic as possible.

I am indebted to my husband and best friend, Victor Shtern (a.k.a. Tolya Dargis), who was by my side all these years, always patient and encouraging, despite my unbearable disposition.

Leaving Leningrad

Prologue

From the day we applied to emigrate from the Soviet Union time seemed to stand still, although according to the calendar it flew like crazy. Four months must have gone by, but in my mind they converged into one exhausting endless day filled with fear that we would be allowed to leave and horror that we would not.

The family fell to pieces. My husband, Anatoly, lay flat in bed with a 104° temperature and no other symptoms.

My mother, usually so neat and smart, sat on the sofa in her bathrobe, her hair disheveled, rocking back and forth like an old Jew in prayer, repeating monotonously: "No, I'm not leaving, not ever. Why should I? Who is going to make me? My whole life is here . . . For no reason at all . . . I am not moving . . . not anywhere . . . never . . ." My heart responded to these quiet murmurs with mixed feelings of anger, tenderness, repentance, and guilt.

My daughter, Katya, then fourteen, turned to stone. For hours she sat on the windowsill, unable to come to her senses after a humiliating school meeting at which her classmates, led by teachers and the school principal, branded her as a traitor, someone who traded the red banners of Russia for the red deserts of the State of Israel. For the sake of fairness it must be noted that an official of the district party committee lent a helping hand to the selfish little girl, offering her a chance to condemn her parents and stay in the only true family—that of the people of the Soviet Union. But the callous child answered, "No way."

Anatoly's colleagues breathed fire and fury. They wrote a letter to the U.S.S.R. Ministry of Foreign Affairs with a bizarre request, "On no condition should Anatoly Dargis be allowed back into the Soviet Union when he becomes disillusioned with the 'capitalist paradise' and begs to come back."

Our building superintendent acted nobly, having written in his testimonial about my mother that "N. P. Verkhovskaya did not disrupt or violate house rules during her entire occupancy of the apartment No. —— ."

My employers behaved quite mysteriously; they actually praised me. "Tatyana Dargis is a talented and competent specialist, hard working, disciplined, and politically correct," they wrote. I suspect that they confused me with some patriotic Communist, some iron comrade who probably was sent to the Congo to help build the tallest dam in the world. I preserved this testimonial in the hope that it would aid me in finding a professional job in the United States or Canada.

What else can I recall about those never-ending times? Suddenly the number of my friends dwindled, falling into three groups—those who vanished and did not call at all, those who called only from roadside pay phones, and those who sat with us for hours in our kitchen, trying to share the burden of our hardship.

And, as a final touch, I remember a fireworks display like a good-bye salute to us by our Motherland.

At some point during that time, Mr. Donald Sheehan, then the U.S. cultural attaché in Leningrad, visited us. The next morning I ran errands and returned home around two o'clock. On the staircase a bitter, suffocating smell hit me, stinging my eyes. The door to our apartment was covered with shreds of blackened insulation and charred felt. Partially burned wet newspapers and magazines were scattered in black puddles on the landing. Afraid to come near my door, I banged on our neighbor's door.

"My God, what happened?"

"A fire. Don't you see?" Zhora Utkin, a metalworker at the Bolshevik factory, explained calmly. "Thank God I work the graveyard shift today, otherwise our places would be . . . phew! Your family is huddled in the far corner of your apartment, scared out of their wits. About an hour ago I smelled an awful stench and ran outside. Your door was in flames. Some 'friends' of yours had stacked a bunch of burning papers and magazines outside your door. I was going to call the fire department. But then I thought, well, to hell with them! They'd only make it stink more and ruin your books with that acid they use, so I put it out myself. Then I ran out to the drugstore and got some Valium for your mother."

"What should I do, Zhora, call the police?"

"What for? What do you need the police for, just think about it—what will they tell you? Do you really think they don't know about it? Or that they give a damn? Can't you see that you are being warned not to mingle with foreigners?"

Later, when I ran into former friends, relations, and colleagues, I read a mute question in their eyes: "What was it that you've been lacking here?" It would be easier for me to list the things that I had in abundance.

If history repeats itself, I thought, and God leads us Jews out of Egypt again, the charred door of my apartment will be the last thing I'll remember as I leave my homeland forever.

1 Birth

What are the main events in a person's life? Birth and death, no doubt. Since it would be a little unconventional to start the story of my life with my death, I'll take the more traditional route and will tell you about my birth.

On the day I was born, the Union of Soviet Socialist Republics, which at that time encompassed one-sixth of all dry land on the globe, was splendidly decorated. Printed slogans, posters, and huge portraits of gloomy men with square shoulders and low foreheads littered the gigantic spaces of my homeland from the capital city of Moscow down to the tiniest villages that aren't even on the map. The color scheme was predominantly red. Military marches drowned all the other sounds. As for smells . . . Well, suffice it to say that the two-hundred-thousand-strong nation was drinking vodka like alcoholics unanimous. Was all that in my honor? Not exactly. The day happened to be May 1, International Labor Day.

When Americans, my new compatriots, ask me the astrological question, "Under what sign of the Zodiac were you born?" I answer out of politeness, "Taurus." But the truth is that I was born under the "Sign of the Four." A huge banner with the profiles of the Great Four—Marx, Engels, Lenin, and Stalin—was hovering atop the Leningrad Institute of Obstetrics and Gynecology, where my mother was to give birth to me.

On that May Day, the doctors and nurses in the hospital did not abstain from joining in the celebrations. They gathered in the internship ward, drinking ethyl alcohol and munching on marinated smelts. They tolerated my mother's cries for a while, but when they eventually got to her they saw that I was stuck in the birth canal, demonstrating inappropriate reluctance to be born. I still wonder what tool they finally chose to pull me out—a crowbar, a shoehorn, or maybe sugar tongs—but as they yanked me out head first they slightly twisted my face into a semi-pretzel shape.

And so, amid the full swing of a national celebration, I arrived in this world with a smashed look that in medical circles is known as "unilateral facial paralysis." A nurse rinsed me off in a chipped basin and showed me to my mother.

"My goodness, what a wretched sight! She is so ugly!" poor Mama whispered in horror.

"You're not such a beauty yourself!" the nurse snapped, pressing me to her ample bosom.

Actually that was not true. Both of my parents were quite handsome and could count on producing a decent-looking offspring. Even as a newborn I apparently was offended and disgusted by my mother's remark. Moreover, I'm certain that this episode, interpreted in the light of modern psychoanalysis, was and still remains the cause of a lifelong clash between my mother and me.

Now I ought to explain a few major differences between Soviet and American hospitals. In the Soviet hospitals, fathers are absolutely forbidden from being present when their babies are born. They are not even allowed to visit their wives and brand-new babies inside the hospital walls. The reason for this rule is strictly hygienic. Hospital administrators are paranoid about viruses and bacteria that fathers and grandparents could easily bring along from the outside world. Therefore a crowd of relatives invariably gathers in the lobby downstairs, sending up notes, fruit, cakes, and flowers with all imaginable viruses and bugs inside and outside the envelopes, packages, and bouquets.

To spare my father's feelings, my mother didn't let him know how really hideous their long-awaited newborn looked. When my father finally came to pick us up a week later, clutching a lavish bouquet of roses, he didn't know what to expect as he raised a corner of the silky baby blanket. Petrified, I stiffened and cringed, expecting yet another insult, but instead tears of admiration glistened behind Papa's spectacles.

"My little beauty!" he whispered.

"Thank God, my dad is nearsighted," I thought, and, breathing a big sigh of relief, I fell asleep.

For the first three months of my life, I could have posed as a model for Salvador Dali. The right side of my face was white and dead. My right cheek drooped, my right eye was sealed. My lips on the right side were pressed tight, and I couldn't even fully open my mouth to cry. The left side of my face was a healthy pink and was able to express my pains and joys. My father's salary was siphoned into the pockets of the medical stars. They would come, look me over, shrug their shoulders, and shake their heads. They had no consoling words.

Once my mother's aunt Pauline, a pediatrician, came from Siberia for a visit. She was a loud, sloppy, and optimistic chain smoker. She hardly said hello, burst into my bedroom without knocking, and froze by my crib, staring at me. Then she poked her tobacco stained fingers in my face, bent all my limbs, and turned to my parents.

"Throw out all her medications. Stop walking around with tragic faces. This ugly duckling will be a beauty someday. Mark my word."

It happened on the day of her departure. I screamed. Pauline choked on a mouthful of strudel and dropped her cup of tea on the floor. "Do you hear? Do you hear HOW she cries? Listen, it's round. Her cry is round."

Everyone rushed to me. I was yelling at the top of my lungs, and my mouth wasn't a crooked, narrow crack any longer but round like a capital letter O.

"Come on, baby, more." Pauline pinched me and pulled my nose until I went into a real frenzy. "Smart girl." With her Siberian strength she scooped me up, and I shut up immediately, gazing out at the world for the very first time with two wide-open eyes.

However, my "childhood disease of Leftism" never really vanished completely. I was always left-handed and left-footed. My view of the world shifted more and more to the left, until I couldn't stand the looks of the "Sign of the Four" anymore. Emigration was the only solution.

Now it should be kept in mind that in Russia we so-called dissidents were considered to be left wing. But when I crossed the Atlantic Ocean I discovered, to my great surprise, that in the West I wasn't left wing at all but—would you believe it—quite right wing!

But let's go back to my childhood. "What do you want to be when you grow up?" I heard this question for the first time when I was three years old and many times after that. I have asked myself this question time and time again, and even now, in my twilight years, I'm still not quite sure. But my first inclination was toward poetry.

I composed my first poem at the age of thirteen. We had gone to Moscow to celebrate my birthday, which coincided, you remember, with May Day. My father's friend, a high-level official, took me to a military parade as a birthday treat. Comrade Stalin, the last of the Great Four, stood on the tribune of Lenin's mausoleum, with the body of comrade Lenin himself, another member of the Great Four, lying inside, beneath him. Suddenly, a strong wave of creative ecstasy burst from me, resulting in the following lines:

> Dearest Stalin, our beloved
> Teacher, father and brother,
> You greet us from the tomb
> In the summer heat, and at the same time
> In the rain, snow and sleet
> And we're endlessly grateful
> That you allow us to be born,
> To breathe, to live, and finally to die!!

Unbeknownst to my parents, I sent my poem to the official children's paper, *Lenin's Sparkle,* and it was published!

A very wary look appeared on my father's face when, taking off his glasses and bringing the newspaper close to his eyes, he read my poem out loud. "Congratulations," Mama said with a sadness incomprehensible to me. "We've raised our own Soviet poetess laureate." And my shy muse fell silent and faded away. Except for minor poetic spurts that overcame me during school romances. As for prose, there was honestly nothing much to write about.

I grew up in an ordinary communal apartment, studied in an ordinary secondary school and then in a second-rate university. I worked in a boring design bureau with a name that consisted of eleven hissing consonants. I defended my boring thesis on "The Structure and Texture of Weak Soils." My only accomplishments in life were that I got married to Tolya Dargis and gave birth to a wonderful daughter, Katya. "Not so bad," you would say, but I was too young and too restless to fully appreciate my life. Rather, I continued to move inexorably toward retirement, dying of boredom.

I had no passions in my life except for the passion with which I hated my job. Nothing ever happened to me that deserved to be immortalized. I didn't fulfill a single Communist dream. I never climbed the Stalin Peak in the Pamir Mountains, lugging along a marble bust of Lenin, or the Lenin Peak in the Caucasus, pressing a bust of Stalin to my heart. I wasn't lucky enough to get my arms and legs frostbitten while exploring the North Pole. I didn't make a round-trip or even a one-way trip into outer space. A dull stream of colorless years passed as I was being dragged along like an empty can. All sorts of Soviet heroes were quacking on the radio, waving from magazine covers, applauding one another in conference halls, but those were not the kind of heroes I was tempted to emulate.

Finally, something really important did happen. At the end of 1976, sick and tired of the Great Four and their ideological followers, I left my home and the country of my birth, crossed the Atlantic Ocean, and landed in the United States of America. Eight months later, I found myself employed by a company with a name even less pronounceable than the eleven Russian hissing consonants. And once again, life was bypassing me.

Obvious signs of depression appeared: insomnia, crying fits, and an irresistible urge to pick a bone with my husband or mother. What would I have done if I had been home in Leningrad? Gone to a shrink? No way, never. I would have called my friend Natasha, or Nina, or Olga. I would have rushed to one of them in a taxi at 1:30 in the morning. (We Russians insist on this particular time when we brag to Americans about the depth and inviolability of our friendships.) We would drink vodka as I cried my heart out to my friend. Around five o'clock in the morning it would become apparent that my troubles were nothing compared to hers. Having comforted Natasha, or Nina, or Olga, I would part with her till the next emotional crisis.

Until very recently the Russian people were afraid to see psychiatrists; the very reference to such a visit in one's medical record could spell trouble for the rest of one's life. If one disagreed with Soviet ideology, so-called corrective psychiatry could be applied, during which the dissident would be institutionalized and subjected to forced psychiatric treatment. Times have changed, however. According to the latest statistics, people of the fallen empire no longer hesitate to go to shrinks. Here is what my old nanny wrote to me: "Vanya, my nephew, has become a complete alcoholic. He went to a psychiatric clinic. The doctor was kind, talked to him for a while, and prescribed some pills. Vanya ate the pills and came back for more, but the doctor was already dead, may he rest in peace. He hung himself during a drinking spree. But Vanya is too ashamed to go to another doctor and now drinks worse than ever."

I decided to see a shrink. Dr. Vincent Rodriguez was short and bald, with an unruly salt-and-pepper mustache. "What has been troubling you?" he asked in a velvety baritone.

"Everything," I said, suppressing a lump in my throat. "First, I have frequent headaches."

"Just think, I do too," answered the doctor as he rubbed his temples.

"Second, I'm feeling irritable and disgusted with my family and friends."

"And how about 'Oh God, I'm getting old?'"

I nodded, overwhelmed by his astuteness. Dr. Rodriguez enumerated all my other symptoms and diagnosed my illness: "There is nothing really wrong with you," he said, "just a banal case of JWM/MAC Syndrome."

"My God, what is it?"

"Jewish Women's Mania and Middle Age Crisis. It's very common. I will put you on Prozac and advise you to do something positive and constructive. Can you remember what you wanted to do when you were, say, five years old?"

"Oh, that's easy. I wanted to be a writer."

"An excellent idea and, truly, very positive. Go for it!"

I went to the drugstore to get my Prozac and also bought some paper, thus launching myself on the road to recovery.

Within a couple of weeks I had accomplished a few things:

- Composed and typed out my first short story, which was accepted for publication;
- Sang an aria from *Rigoletto* while washing dishes;
- In response to Mother's usual "Put your coat on, it's rather nippy today," didn't bark back but answered, smiling, "I'm not cold"; and
- Upon seeing my husband's socks strewn all over the living room, did not have a crying fit and instead quietly threw them into the hamper.

Other miraculous signs of recovery appeared. The strongest among them was the overwhelming desire to write about my life. And thus this book was conceived.

2 Ancestors and Relatives

My family tree cannot be traced too far and doesn't contain any names worth mentioning. Yet I must tell you about my grandfather and my Uncle Pavel, who played important roles in my life.

My maternal grandfather, Pavel Romanovich Kramer, was a well-known engineer in pre-Revolutionary St. Petersburg who used to know Vladimir Lenin and even corresponded with him. Curiously, I never used this fact to climb the Soviet social ladder. Anyway, my grandfather and Lenin were acquainted. While Gramps was vacationing at a resort in Basel, Switzerland, he dabbled in music-making and spent his evenings playing romantic Russian music on the piano in the same hotel where Lenin was staying. One day the great founder of the world's first Communist country came into the lounge, leaned on the top of the piano, and dreamily murmured some lyrics to the music. Both Grandfather and Lenin were deeply moved by this experience, being fellow countrymen from St. Petersburg.

Later they drank beer together and took leisurely walks along the narrow, sleepy streets of Basel. No doubt, during their conversations Lenin shared with my grandfather his ideas about the theory and practice of the Revolution. Before they went their separate ways they exchanged addresses. I don't know which address Mr. Lenin gave to Mr. Kramer (perhaps that of his legendary secret cabin in the forest, where he was hiding from the Tzar's police), but Grandfather truly did receive four or five short letters from the great leader.

This acquaintance must have left an indelible impression on my grandfather, because a year after the Revolution he left Russia in a hurry, taking with him his wife, two children, and three suitcases. His son, Pavel, was five years old at the time; his daughter, Natasha (my future mother), was fifteen. Little Pavel, as his age would indicate, held no political views. However, Natasha (or Tatusya, as she was nicknamed in the family) was rather rebellious. Somewhere south of Riga, where surging groups of railroad staff lingered along the side-tracks, awaiting their pickup, Tatusya slipped out of the train car and vanished. Not wanting to be cut off from the tumultuous events in the making of Russian history, my future mother hid in a freight car with Latvian soldiers and returned to St. Petersburg (by this time called Petrograd). The next time she saw her fragmented family was fifty years later.

My grandparents and their son followed the traditional route of the first wave of Russian emigrants: Berlin, Paris, and then to the New World. In Paris, my Uncle Pavel, transformed into Paul, became obsessed with the cinema and traversed the thorny path from being a lighting engineer to a film director. In 1940, he and his parents went to Lisbon, Portugal, to escape the Nazis. On the way they were robbed of all their belongings, including what was left of their money and jewelry. Grandfather had a stroke and Grandmother went nearly blind. Paul was left with his helpless parents on his hands.

As he wandered around Lisbon he wracked his brain over how he was going to feed his parents and get money for tickets and visas to the States. One lucky day, over an aperitif in a bar, he struck up a conversation with a respectable-looking gentleman. This accidental companion turned out to be a businessman who also was in love with the cinema. As a hobby, he had shot a feature film, but he had no idea of how to market it.

Uncle Paul listened with great attention to his long and sad tale and, at the first pause, assumed an air of importance. "This is your lucky day," he said. After dropping a few famous names, Paul told the man that in a matter of days he would be sailing to America, where Paramount Pictures had practically collapsed in his absence. "I'll do the publicity for your film," he continued. "With my connections, there should be no problem. Of course, some money will be needed for the arrangements, but we are business people. We know that these expenses will more than pay for themselves."

The next day Paul received from the businessman several rolls of film in a metal box and a large sum of money. Unaccustomed to swindling, Uncle Paul suffered great pangs of conscience. The day before his scheduled departure, with the tickets and visas in his pocket, he appeared before his savior and confessed. The businessman was moved to tears.

"My dear boy, bon voyage, and may God be with you. If only I had such a devoted son I would be very proud."

It sounds like a fairy tale with a happy ending, though the real happy ending came later. Uncle Paul made a very successful career in the cinema, and he actually did show that film in twenty-four of the American states, thus earning back all the money to repay his benefactor.

My introduction to Uncle Paul took place in Leningrad, almost thirty years later. One day in 1968, there was a long-distance phone call.

"May I speak with Tatusya, please?"

The voice was unfamiliar and the pronunciation too precise. Besides, no one had called my mother Tatusya for years.

"Who is speaking?"

"This is her brother Paul, please."

"Ma!" I bellowed from the hallway. "Some kind of psycho wants to talk to you."

Never once had the thought that an Uncle Paul existed on this planet occurred to me. Any contacts with relatives abroad were extremely dangerous for the Soviet people, and those who had them preferred to forget about them.

"Hello," Mama said in her deep contralto. There was a pause, then a hysterical cry, and she banged the receiver back on the hook. I dashed off for some Valium, but the phone rang again.

"Listen," I said, "are you really Mama's brother? How did you find us? Where are you calling from?"

"I'm in Moscow, at the Hotel Ukraine. And I had no problem locating you. I just mentioned Tatusya's maiden name to certain . . . well . . . certain comrades. But with whom am I speaking?"

"With Tatusya's daughter. My name is Tanya."

"How exciting! Are you a big girl now?"

"Bigger than I'd like to be. But let me get your sister for you."

Mother was still sobbing, so I took the matter into my own hands.

"Listen Paul, I'll bring your sister to her senses, take her to the airport, and send her off on the first flight to Moscow. She will go to the Hotel Ukraine and call you from the lobby. What is your number?"

"Sounds wonderful, but there is no need. I'm flying to Leningrad tomorrow."

Twenty-four hours before Uncle's arrival our home was in a whirl. I called my boss and in a weak voice said that a severe back pain would leave me bedridden for about a week. Then I called my husband, Anatoly, at work and ordered him to put his bullshit (that's what we called his experiments on the superconductivity of liquid helium) on hold and go get our former nanny, Nulya, to clean up the apartment and make her famous *pelmeni* (small meat ravioli). And then I began calling friends and acquaintances who had access to the traditional Russian delicacies—beluga caviar, smoked salmon, and sturgeon. My mother took no part in these proceedings. Rather, she lay in bed surrounded by Uncle's baby pictures, hot water bottles, and heart pills.

Paul arrived in the Soviet Union as the head of an ABC network television crew to shoot a joint Soviet-American documentary film, "Stars of Soviet Sports." It took the Soviet Agency of Printed News, APN, two years to prepare for the project. During that time, different "comrades" met with Paul in New York to decide whom, where, and how they were to shoot. Afraid to tempt Providence, Paul never mentioned during those meetings the fact that his only sister lived somewhere in the Soviet Union (if she was still alive, God willing). But after arriving in Moscow and putting his suitcases in the lobby of the Hotel Ukraine, he made it clear that no shooting could begin until he found his sister, who in 1917 had been living in Petrograd (Leningrad) at such and such address.

The "comrades" did their homework and looked for us, although we didn't know it at the time. But I remembered later that a few days prior to Uncle's call several people had visited our apartment under various pretexts, though their visits did not seem significant at the time. One was a telephone repairman who replaced the phone cord; another, an unusually sober plumber who fixed the leaking toilet tank. Even the building superintendent dropped in. He complimented us on our kitchen furniture, inquired about my mother's health, and, with a mysterious grin, departed. Our living standards must have satisfied some high-level officials, and so Paul was given our address and phone number.

Uncle turned out to be a youthful-looking gentleman in his early fifties with curly silver hair and smiling eyes. He was dressed in suede from head to toe, smoked strong Camel cigarettes, and seemed electrified by excess energy. We all were amused by the striking physical resemblance and other similarities between brother and sister. They both adored liver pâté, Roquefort cheese, and olives. Both were heavy smokers, were indifferent to classical music, but considered the Argentine tango the height of musical achievement. Both danced a mean Charleston and believed the cinema to be the highest form of human creativity. Mother was once a star of the silent screen and then wrote scripts for a popular science television series for many years, until a new generation of arrogant young upstarts replaced her in the studio. But most surprising was Uncle's fluent Russian, for he immediately grasped both the humor and the most recent nuances of city slang. He would have been practically indistinguishable from one of us except that every detail of Soviet life completely bewildered him.

"Why don't you have checkbooks? It makes life so much easier."

"What do you mean you don't get unemployment benefits? What do people live on when they lose their jobs?"

"How can one choose a car or a brand of shampoo if there are no commercials?"

We patiently explained to Paul the unique aspects of the transitional period from Socialism to Communism. We, in turn, could not get over the credit cards and drivers' licenses that, in Uncle's country, replaced every conceivable identification card, including the passport.

On a more personal note, we learned that Paul was a widower and the father of a seventeen-year-old son, Bertrand. His wife, a French actress, had died from throat cancer ten years earlier at the age of thirty-two. Easily changing roles from that of older sister to mother-protector, my mother reproached Paul for not remarrying, describing the horrors of a lonely old age. Uncle assured us that he was taking well to single life. He had a Swedish girlfriend by the name of Ula, and they were thinking of traveling together. She lived in Stockholm, worked as a translator, and was actually planning to travel to the Soviet Union. Uncle produced some photographs from his pocket, and we duly admired the tall blond with sensuous lips.

Then the entire film crew came to our home accompanied by KGB agents masquerading as Russian "consultants." The phone rang off the hook, *pelmeni* were cooked and gobbled by the hundreds, the glorious smell of Ukrainian borsch permeated the apartment, and a pile of empty vodka bottles was growing on the floor. Packs of Kent and Marlboro, Uncle's jackets, and colorful plastic bags were scattered everywhere. Paul was shooting his film during the day, spent the evenings at our place, and returned to the Hotel Astoria in the wee hours of the morning.

On the fifth day Paul awoke to a strange mumbling and opened his eyes to see two "consultants" from APN in his brightly lit hotel room. It was three o'clock in the morning.

"We do not seem to be able to get any sleep," comrade Volkov confided. "We saw that your room was not locked, so we decided you weren't able to sleep either, Pavel Pavlovich." (Obviously, the Russian version of my uncle's name lent intimacy to their international collaboration.)

"Now I definitely cannot get to sleep," said my astonished uncle.

"Very good," the comrades rejoiced. "Since none of us can get any sleep, let's have a drink—to your long-lost and finally found Soviet family."

Two bottles of Stolichnaya and a small can of black caviar appeared on the table. A disoriented Paul pulled on his pajamas, gulped down half a glass of vodka, and, imitating the drinking customs of his new friends, took a whiff of his pajama sleeve.

"Just think," comrade Zaytsev said dreamily, "you have found your family again. And what a family! Your sister is still a beauty. Probably you did not expect to find her alive and well. And your niece? She's fine looking, and a geologist to boot. And just look at her husband, Anatoly, with a doctorate in physics and math! In what other country can you accomplish so much? And their little daughter Katya, your granddaughter once removed in a sense, she goes to an English school. It's not just a family, it's f— royalty!"

"I am quite happy and very proud of them," Uncle confirmed.

"So are we!" chimed in the Greek chorus of "consultants," but then Comrade Volkov became sad. "Is it not horrible that fate has split all of you up? If only you could reunite; that would be my advice."

"What do you mean? In the States?" In the face of such a delicate question Uncle Paul reverted to his more familiar English.

"What has the States got to do with it? Why not stay here with us, that is, with them?" asked Comrade Zaytsev, his eyes moistening as he hugged Uncle. "We will write at once to inform your boy. How old is he, seventeen?"

"That's right," Uncle confirmed.

Outside the window of the Hotel Astoria, the colonnade of Saint Isaac's Cathedral radiated a cool serenity in the spring night. Comrade Zaytsev seated himself on the windowsill, blocking out a dark-lilac sky.

"Isn't it just terrible to be left a widower at the age of forty?" he said, demonstrating how well informed he was. "It's awful how people in these days are dying off from cancer."

Now it was Uncle's turn to be sorrowful. He showed some photos of his late wife.

"The picture of beauty!" Volkov and Zaytsev declared in unison.

"And here is my little boy." From the photo a sly face with round eyes smiled back.

"Why, he's a chip off the old block!" APN assured Paul.

"He takes after my side of the family. He has quite a talent for filmmaking."

"What about VGIK? He should enroll in our famous VGIK!" responded Volkov with staggering alacrity, referring to the State Institute of Cinematography. "The best film institute in the world! Just ask Fellini! And your son will have absolutely no problem getting accepted, we will see to that. Dear Pavel Pavlovich, in our country all roads will be open to you, trust us."

Although the vodka had noticeably gone to Uncle's head, he moved on, carefully navigating the hidden political reefs.

"Thank you, dear friends," said Paul. "Your idea, surprising as it is, is very flattering. Of course, I must think about it carefully before I make such an important decision."

"Think, Pavel Pavlovich, think positively and try to give us an answer in the next couple of days. In the meantime, don't let us keep you from your sleep." Zaytsev and Volkov bowed ceremoniously and left Uncle's room.

A week passed by and Paul still had not come to a "positive" decision. That late night visit had led his thoughts along a completely different line.

"It's not such a bad idea, after all. Why don't you emigrate?"

"Paul!" my mother exclaimed. "Come to your senses!"

"This is out of the question, Uncle," I said. "I have a thesis to defend soon."

"Defend it in New York. An American degree from an American university is not worth any less than a Soviet one."

"Bravo! How clever of you! And just who do you think will allow us to leave?"

"Isn't anyone interested in my opinion?" Anatoly asked. "I think that this is nothing but madness and meaningless rubbish." He pointed silently to the telephone. "And, by the way, couldn't we take a walk and discuss the matter outside of these walls?"

Mama walked up to the phone, put a pencil in the dial, and covered the phone with a pillow as well.

"I ran away from the family and fought for this country, so that . . ."

"Haven't you had enough of the Revolution?" Paul interrupted his sister. "After your stories I can't sleep at night. You have been married twice, and both of your husbands have disappeared in prison camps."

"Times have changed, dear."

"That's a great relief. Yet the whole time I'm here I feel some kind of invisible but heavy weight pressing down on me. It's as if somebody is watching me day and night."

"Just think, Uncle Paul," our eight-year-old daughter, Katya, piped up, "when you and Grandma dropped by to pick me up at school, the kids in our class knew right away that you were a foreigner."

"You probably bragged about him," Anatoly said.

"No, honestly I didn't. I said, how do you know? And they said that he looks like he couldn't care less about anything."

"How very flattering . . . Tatusya, you are living in some kind of dream world where you don't really see what is going on. Meanwhile these so-called consultants follow me around, they have the nerve to come into my room in the middle of the night, and they are constantly interfering with the shooting of my own film."

"Darling, don't get so upset. They'd obviously brainwashed you in the States," Mama said. "I never cease to be amazed at how much freedom you are given here."

"Fine, but listen to this. Between shootings I have a habit of filming with my own camera whatever interests me, and many things capture my interest. Yesterday the camera and all the films disappeared from my room. Naturally, I made a big fuss."

"Why don't you ever tell us things like this?"

"This is precisely what I'm doing now. Anyway, I made a scene, and the administration of the Astoria called a police captain. What a farce! He went through my suitcases, checked under the mattress, behind the heater, and even poked the toilet with a stick. And do you know what he said? 'Your camera was stolen by some Finns. Our people have not been stealing here for a long time now. But if some Soviet citizen is involved in this, we will get him, rest assured.' And his look was so ominous that I began to wonder whether I was this thief, whether I had not taken it myself."

"You know, Paul," Anatoly said nervously, "it is getting rather late. Let us walk you back to the hotel, and we can talk on the way." He looked sideways at the phone.

"The pencil and pillow are not all that reliable, eh?" Uncle chuckled sadly.

We went outside. The city was asleep, the damp streets were deserted after the rain. Someone was playing the guitar in the park in front of the Hotel Astoria.

"I'm not trying to talk you into anything. Life in America is certainly not easy, and we have massive problems. But these problems are those of a normal, functioning society, not a concentration camp where the prisoners and the guards are afraid of each other. I am not too fluent in Russian, but I see that here a synonym of the word 'government' is 'power.' I always hear: 'Soviet power' forbids this, or 'Soviet power' permits that . . . I cannot imagine that anybody in America would ever use the word 'power' synonymously with 'government' or 'administration,' even by mistake."

Paul lifted his head and pointed to a window on the second floor. "You see? That is my window. It's dark, I'm still not home. But the neighboring one is lit. That means the 'comrades' are waiting for me to discuss political asylum with them. My God! For fifty years I suffered from nostalgia, yet I've been cured of it in the course of one week. How simple it has turned out to be, and how sad."

We have never seen Uncle's film. Apparently Paul, while shooting the soccer match at Luzhniki Stadium, filmed the soccer fans, who looked sullen and drunk. He proceeded to "distort Soviet reality" during the shooting of Georgian horsemen in Tbilisi, "slandered" the Baltic Regatta, "smeared" the apartment of the world champion high jumper Valery Brumel, and made a "dirty hint" about two sister-athletes, Tamara and Irina Press, who turned out to be either hermaphrodites or outright men. And so the film about Soviet sport stars was censored in the homeland of those very stars.

3 The Carrot and the Stick

Paul flashed like a shooting star through the dim expanse of our lives and disappeared, leaving traces in the shape of Dior perfumes, bottles of Courvoisier, a case of Marlboros, and other tokens of a different, glamorous world. Our parting day was full of sorrow. Our entire family went to Moscow to see him off. Now that her brother was finally found after having been lost for half a century, Mama would not let go of his hand. When the boarding call was announced, Paul smiled at us timidly and vanished into the bowels of the Sheremetyevo Airport. His Moscow–New York flight took off into the gray sky as we trudged back to our uneventful life.

Soon, various reminders of Uncle's generosity began to knock at our door. Now a visiting American would call with gifts and greetings, a package would arrive in the mail. Our shelves became brightly littered with western art books and Beatles records. Closets were filling up with leather goods, the family was decked out in blue jeans, and I donned a new, full-length sheepskin coat.

"Oh, we are really going to get it now," lamented Anatoly, who was known for his pragmatic mind and a realistic approach to life that made him a real "wet blanket" and a bore. "Nothing good will come of these international contacts."

"Oh, come on. Good Lord, who would ever want any of us?" I brushed him off. "Don't be a pain in the neck again."

Spring tulips gave way to a rainy summer, and golden leaves to frost-covered trees. Tolya's prediction still had not come true. Then one day I had a call at work.

"Good day, Tatyana Sergeevna. Could you drop in for a minute to the First Department?" The voice was smooth and sweet as honey, yet hard and sharp as a steel blade.

"Hello, who is this?"

"This is Soprikin here. Sorry to disturb you."

I hate to be disturbed at work, particularly by the First Department.

"What happened, Mr. Soprikin?"

"We'd just like to have a little chat. Try to drop by right now. It won't be for long."

"Well, if it is for just a minute. I have a customer coming in half an hour."

What on earth did he need? The First Department (found in every establishment, be it a factory, a university, or a hospital) is responsible for the keeping and distribution of classified materials and information. It also makes sure that employees who work with classified material never have any contacts with foreigners. All my life I'd been trying to keep as far away as possible from anything classified.

A narrow, dusty corridor lined with numerous iron-plated doors led to the First Department. Some of the doors had engraved plates: "Distribution of Materials: 9–12 A.M.; Returning: 3–5 P.M."; "Leave briefcases and bags on the table outside"; "Leave coats at the door"; or "Authorized Personnel Only."

Since I had a coat and a bag but no authorization, I stopped to think which door to avoid the most. At this very moment the door marked "Authorized Personnel Only" opened slightly to reveal a slender man I'd never seen before. He held out his hand and, with the words "Tatyana Sergeevna, please do come in," stepped aside to let me through.

I was barely able to suppress a gasp of astonishment: the interior was most unusually elegant for a small company such as ours. Violet velvet curtains with heavy pleats draped down to the floor to conceal the boiler-house and the venereal disease clinic outside the window. Oval armchairs surrounded a table sparkling like a skating rink, with two crystal glasses, a bottle of mineral water, a bowl of oranges, and a box of the finest chocolates. The green eye of a radio flickered in the corner as it filled the room with languidly mournful sounds of piano music.

The stranger closed the door and locked it. At that very moment the rat-like face of Comrade Soprikin, the head of the First Department, poked out from an inner door.

"Oh, you have found each other." He grinned and disappeared. Another lock clicked shut.

"Allow me to take your coat," said the young man, locking an enchanted gaze on my sheepskin coat. "Now let me introduce myself."

He produced an identification card from his pocket and held it up under my nose. I managed to read and memorize his rank—"Captain of the KGB"—and a long enough first name and patronymic, "Stanislav Feodorovich." But I did not have time to catch his last name. Was there a last name on the identification at all?

"Please, have a seat," said the captain, pulling out an armchair. "Do you smoke?"

He took out a pack of Kents and tapped the bottom. Two cigarettes darted out like soldiers in formation.

"Why do you suppose we are having this meeting, Tatyana Sergeevna?"

"I have not the slightest idea," I said, pressing my hand to my cheek in an attempt to stop the uncontrollable tic in my left eye and the left corner of my lips.

"Take a guess . . ." The chocolates smoothly slid over to my elbow.

"I don't have a clue," I said, shrugging my shoulders, "what about me could have attracted the attention of the KGB."

"Don't be so cautious and reserved. I just want to get to know you."

My head was throbbing from tension and fear; my veins either snapped or tied up in knots. Never in my life had I experienced such a massive migraine.

". . . Concluding this morning's concert was Chopin's Nocturne. At 1:15 we will listen to the program on Quality and Standards," the green eye of the radio crooned in the corner.

The captain leaned back in his chair, successfully imitating the smile of Mona Lisa.

"Tatyana Sergeevna," he said at last, "are you familiar with the name Ula Werner?"

Ula . . . Ula Werner . . . I shook my pulsating head.

"Think carefully now, and do not rush. You must know this name."

Ula . . . Ula . . . Ula . . . Oh, Lord, of course! Uncle Paul's girlfriend . . . That was all I knew about Ula . . . practically nothing.

"Yes, Comrade Captain, that is the name of an acquaintance of my mother's brother."

"You will please call me Stanislav Feodorovich, all right? So, the name is familiar to you. Excellent. Could you describe her appearance?"

"I have never seen her."

"You have seen pictures of her. Characterize her. Give me a verbal description."

"I cannot remember."

"Anything in the most general terms will do."

"I can say nothing about her."

"You are being stubborn for no reason," the captain said and began to drum out a steady beat on the table, for the first time indicating that he was annoyed. "Could you at least identify her?"

"What do you mean?"

"Could you recognize Ula Werner if you met her in some public place?"

"Of course not."

"Do not be so certain. Picture yourself in the following scenario: In front of you are twenty or thirty people, and it is known that she is among them. How about then?"

Good Lord, what is he getting at? What does he want from me? Don't ask any questions . . . Don't rush . . . Think before you speak . . . Despite these admonitions to myself, I violated the first law of conduct with the KGB: never, ever, ask any questions.

"What do you need Ula Werner for?"

The captain smoked a second cigarette, which lent his face an expression of deep thought, as if he were considering whether to share State secrets with me. Finally, he said: "You see, Tatyana Sergeevna, she is involved in unethical behavior toward our country. I can explain no further. Now, could you identify her?"

The captain of the KGB, distressed over a violation of ethics! This was something new. The old guard of this organization did not even know the meaning of this word. I took charge of my tic, removed my hand from my cheek, and lit a cigarette.

"I already answered that. I would not be able to identify her."

The captain poured mineral water into the glasses and peeled an orange, carving the rind into an elegant rose. "Please help yourself."

"Thank you, but I'm allergic to oranges."

"Really? Whoever would have thought of such a thing!" The orange was put aside. "Now, to return to our subject." He walked around the room and changed the radio station. The sweet voice of the ethnic singer Muslim Magomaev filled the air.

"You must appreciate my trust in you and my openness. We need your help. Ula Werner is coming to Leningrad in a few days. Not alone, but with a group of Swedish tourists. It is not known whether she will call you, but for us it is absolutely essential that the two of you meet. And this meeting must seem as if it were purely coincidental. We will work out all the details." He stood behind my chair and casually bent forward. The acrid smell of his after-shave hit me in the nose.

"I do not understand the point of this meeting."

"Oh, it is nothing, really. For keeping contact, that's all. And you are the most suitable person for the job." He went around the table again and sat down, never taking his eyes off me. "Technically, everything should go very smoothly and naturally."

Technically, everything should go very smoothly and naturally. You will be fulfilling what seems at first a harmless and innocent favor. Then you will be hooked, already entangled in their sticky web as if gripped by strong, steel claws. The next assignment will be more tricky. You will not be able to escape, and there will be nowhere to hide or disappear to. The only thing left to do will be to jump off the Palace Bridge into the Neva River.

"The group will arrive next Wednesday and stay at the Hotel Russia. They will be there at two in the afternoon, and while they're registering, Ula will be downstairs in the lobby for about an hour. You will also turn up there and you will bump into her by accident. You will begin to chat and discover that you have a mutual friend. If you wish, you may invite her to your home."

What does he want Ula for? Does he really need Ula? Not likely. Ula is probably just bait. That means they're really after me. But why? As an international informer perhaps. They know all too well that since Uncle Paul's visit foreigners have been milling about at home . . . Do not panic, all right? Take control of yourself, and do not agree to do anything.

"No, Comrade Captain, this role does not suit me. I have nothing to discuss with your Ula."

"Actually, she is not ours yet," the captain smiled. "But you need not be so modest. Everyone knows how sociable you are, how easily you are able to make contacts and win people over. You are very charming. They say half of the city are friends of yours. Therefore I am not giving you any instructions but simply rely on your intuition and common sense. Is it a deal?"

Everyone knows how sociable you are. *They say* that half of the city are friends of yours . . . That means that one of these friends is a snitch. No doubt he is waiting for a burst of outrage and for me to demand "Who says so?" But I won't take the bait.

"Unfortunately, I can't be of any help to you."

"Even if she herself calls and comes to see you?"

"She will not come because next week no one will be home. We are going away."

"Where to, if it is not a secret?"

"Is this an interrogation?"

"No, of course not. You do not need to say anything if you don't wish to. Still, I would like to know why you are refusing. It is a mere trifle that requires no more than an hour of your time."

"I can't spare even an hour on trifles."

"Ah, so that's it!" The captain raised his voice for the first time. "And if it is not a trifle? If your help would serve our national security?"

Suddenly, for no apparent reason, I felt at ease, as if some omnipotent, invisible being had stroked my cheek with a soft hand, taking away both the pain in my head and that miserable animal fear.

"Comrade Captain, if my country happened to be in danger I would not hesitate to give my life for it. But . . . this is not the case. You can handle this without me."

"It's up to us to decide such things!"

The captain walked up to the window, drew apart the curtains, made sure that the boiler-house was still in its place, and sharply turned back to me.

"Are you familiar with the name Kiril Azovsky?"

Was I ever! Our families have been on good terms since times immemorial. Kiril Azovsky's father taught literature at the high school my father attended. Later, Professor Mikhail Azovsky headed the Department of Russian Folklore Studies at Leningrad University. In Stalinist times he had been branded as a renegade and cosmopolitan, was hounded by the Party Committee, and in the end died of a heart attack. Kiril was then only fifteen. The day after his father died their doorbell rang. Kiril opened the door to find a *troika* (a Party organizer, a Trade Union organizer, and the Dean) standing there, propping up a fifty-pound metal wreath interwoven with a funeral ribbon reading, "To Mikhail Nikolayevich Azovsky from Leningrad University."

"May we come in?" asked the dean.

"No," Kiril said, and, stepping forward, he grabbed the wreath with both hands, lifted it off the floor (where did he find such strength?), and threw it so hard it rolled down the stairs.

Looking across the table, I responded to the captain, "The name of Azovsky is familiar to me, but what does he have to do with anything?"

"Nothing, I just wanted to watch your reaction," the captain said, admiring the noticeable effect of his question. "So, your friend Kiril Azovsky was expelled from graduate school two months before his defense. And do you know why? Because he is hobnobbing with all sorts of scum as long as they are foreigners. All these books, records, songs, and parties . . . simply outrageous! A den of bacchanalians! Such a person should not and will not teach our youth. A Soviet educator is obliged to be not only an academic specialist but a role model as well. Someone with a clear conscience! Do I make myself clear?"

Perfectly clear, I thought. We are now reverting to threats.

On the radio a milkmaid by the name of Nina Bukova was being extolled for milking twenty liters a day from each of her milk-producing cows. Exasperated, the captain pulled the cord, and the green eye flickered out. A silence, which in classic Russian literature would have been called "ominous," settled over the room. I was apparently not the only one who thought so, because the lock clicked and through the crack of the inner door poked the rat's nose of the head of the First Department.

"Is everything all right in there?" comrade Soprikin inquired. "Would you like some more mineral water?"

"Everything is just fine," smiled the captain. "Thank you." The nose disappeared.

"How is that thesis of yours coming along?" the KGB agent asked with the tone of a tired academician. Good-bye salary raise. So long flexible schedule, library days, and long vacations. Looks like four years of my life have just gone down the drain.

"Up until now it had been going quite well."

"When are you planning on your defense?"

"IIASA, in the fall." This abbreviation stands for "If I'm Still Around." That's how Leo Tolstoy used to end all his letters. But the captain seemed livid. The innocent "IIASA" had sounded like a curse to him, and he blushed.

"What did you say?"

"If there are no surprises, then in November."

"Whether there are to be any surprises, as you put it, depends entirely upon you."

There was a pause. The conversation came to a standstill, and I looked at my watch.

"What is your hurry?" The captain leaned back in his chair, took out another cigarette, and flicked his lighter. "Let us suppose that you successfully defend your thesis. And then what? Do you plan merely to rest on your laurels?"

"Better on laurels than on a prison bed," as an old university saying goes, but I kept quiet.

"Why not travel to America to visit your uncle?"

"I was refused permission to go even to Poland to attend a conference!"

"That happens . . . things like that do happen. However, in the future I do not foresee such problems. You help us and we will help you. Ah yes, by the way, you are a theater fan, aren't you? Tickets for any American or European guest performers are practically impossible to get nowadays, but we have reservations everywhere. And so . . . if you have any problems, do not hesitate to give us a call. We can help you get tickets." He wrote his initials, S.F., and a phone number on a slip of paper.

At this juncture I exploded with fury, offended by this indignity and humiliation.

"What kind of cheap trash do you take me for, Comrade Captain? Even if I never once enter any theater until the day I die, I will never think of turning to the KGB for help!"

"Well, well!" the captain was taken aback. "You love us that much, do you? Take this phone number and call me about Ula. I am counting on your help. If I do not hear from you by Sunday, I will personally come after you."

He stood up, gave me my coat, put the key in the lock, and held out his hand as he flashed a charming smile.

"I do not ask you to sign anything, but our conversation should not be made known to a living soul. I strongly recommend that you keep this in mind. See you soon."

The lock clicked, and I again found myself in the dark corridor lined with steel-plated doors. I didn't feel like returning to my office. Instead, I took a walk, trying to make up my mind about two things. First, should I or should I not do the KGB any favors? On the one hand, my professional career was in jeopardy. On the other, did they really need Ula badly enough to ruin my whole life? Second, how serious was the captain's warning to keep my mouth shut? I had to talk to someone, but not to my family. My husband and my mother, like the vast majority of the Soviet people, have always been paranoid about any encounters with the KGB, and my story could cause a couple of heart attacks in the family. But I desperately needed to talk to someone who knew how to handle this situation, to someone who could give me sober advice.

I walked along the Neva embankment, mentally excluding one person after another from the list of close friends and potential confidants. Some I didn't want to involve in this mess, others I didn't trust. Finally, one name came to mind: Vadim Bolshakov. He wasn't my friend but rather was a former student of my late father. In the last few years he had made a dazzlingly successful career at the university, rising to a full professor of history and Party leader of the history department. Rumor had it that during the war Bolshakov had been a Soviet secret agent in Germany and that many years later he still maintained quite close ties with the KGB. He used to be very fond of my father, but I had not seen him since my father's death. Yet I had a gut feeling that he was the right person to talk to. I called him from a public phone.

"What happened?" he asked in place of a greeting when I told him my name.

"I'd like to talk to you."

"Is it urgent?"

"Yes, I think so."

"Can you come to my place?"

"Well . . . I would prefer to meet somewhere else. In the Summer Garden, for instance."

"I'll be there in twenty minutes."

The Summer Garden, one of the city's most beautiful sites, used to be the aristocracy's favorite strolling place before the Revolution. It was like le Jardin Luxembourg in Paris. When I was a little girl my father used to take me to the Summer Garden every Sunday. I loved those long walks along the serene wide alleys lined by centennial oaks and maples and those elegant marble statues of the Roman gods and goddesses. Now I was imagining the shadow of the KGB officer hiding behind every tree and every statue. When finally I saw Bolshakov at the far end of the alley I was ready to cover his face with kisses.

I told Bolshakov about my lost and found Uncle Paul, about the KGB attempt to seduce Paul to ask for political asylum in the Soviet Union, about his mysterious girlfriend Ula Werner, and about my meeting with the KGB officer. Bolshakov was listening with great interest.

"It looks like they are really after you rather than Ula. They can deal with her without your help. I believe they are recruiting you for 'general purposes.'"

"What shall I do?"

"Nothing. Nothing at all."

"Shall I warn Ula?"

"No way. By no means. No contacts with Ula. Disconnect your phone. Better still, take a vacation and vanish for at least a week, until Ula leaves town."

"But how can I? I can't take a vacation now."

"Get sick. Lower back pain. Acute inflammation of the ulcer. Or simply break a leg, or an arm."

"He was almost threatening me that I might never defend my thesis."

"Millions of people manage to survive without a Ph.D."

"But I might lose my job."

"So what? Is it such a high price to pay for a clear conscience? You are asking for my advice. Here it is, Tanya . . . Don't do them any favors. Don't flirt with the KGB." Bolshakov looked at his watch. "Sorry, I have to run. Say hello to your family for me."

He gave me a peck on the cheek, walked away, and disappeared from my life.

4 You Cannot Get There from Here

Two and a half years passed, and I never heard from Captain Stanislav Feodorovich again. Either the KGB decided to leave me alone, or they just forgot about me altogether. Or was I spared by Bolshakov's rescuing hand? I will never know.

I defended my thesis and got my Ph.D. in geology. My American Uncle Paul parted with Ula, married a French woman, and moved to Paris. For my birthday he sent me a recording of Ella Fitzgerald singing "I Love Paris."

Humming this very song one morning in 197 — , I ran down the stairs, late for work as usual. Imagine a dark November morning in Leningrad. The coming day promises to be dreary as usual, payday was still three days away, and the puffed face of our department chief, comrade Pypin, loomed in my mind's eye. What can the mail possibly bring on such a morning?

I opened the mailbox. The magazines *Communist* and *Woman Worker* and a bunch of bills dropped to my feet. Between them I noticed a lilac envelope encrusted with seals and scarlet crests. Uncle Paul was inviting me to visit him in France.

Today many people receive invitations to go abroad. But in 197 — an invitation mailed from the municipality of Paris and sealed with wax surprised me more than a message from a flying saucer would have.

I called my office and, fighting the exultation that was choking me, informed Pypin of a sudden gall bladder attack. "I cannot come to work today."

"Okay. But don't forget to bring a note from your doctor tomorrow."

Half an hour later, I was on my way to OVIR, the Passport and Visa Office. These days the OVIR waiting room is overcrowded, like the Red Square used to be during the Revolution anniversaries. But then, in 197 —— , the OVIR was empty and as silent as a Buddhist temple.

I was interviewed by Comrade Kabashkin, a stout blond man with a face like a copper basin. Producing an imitation of a smile, he motioned to a chair, shoved an ashtray in my direction, and submerged himself in reading my invitation. When Kabashkin finally looked up, his copper basin was glowing softly.

"When would you like to go to Paris?"

I was so overwhelmed by his courteous question that I lost the gift of speech. Such a considerate question caught me off guard because the OVIR's clerks, as well as all other Soviet clerks, are notorious for their rudeness. So I was not prepared for such politeness.

"I don't know . . . as soon as possible, that is . . . as soon as I receive permission . . ." I squeezed out.

"I personally feel that spring is the best time," he said dreamily.

"Spring, you think?"

"Spring, spring . . . Everything is in bloom there then."

Invisible violins began singing; the room filled with the aroma of blooming chestnut and acacia trees. My suspicions melted like March ice on the lake.

"Would it be possible to go sooner? For instance in January?"

"Why not? It's beautiful there in winter, too. Only, I'm not sure they have snow in Paris then. How will you ski?" he asked anxiously.

"I will try to survive without skiing or even skating."

"It's up to you, up to you."

"Will there be time to process my papers?"

"Why not? The tourist season is over, and everything that depends on us will be done on time."

Above his copper basin of a face a golden halo appeared. He carried on a bit longer about Paris, confirming the presence there of the Louvre and the Eiffel Tower, and parted with me reluctantly. In saying good-buy, Kabashkin handed me a few questionnaires: Form No. 6, Form No. 86, and Form No. 1003, eight copies each.

"I hope you will be able to fill out the questionnaires without any difficulty. The sooner the better. And don't forget twelve passport-size pictures."

The pile of forms was so thick I had to hold it in both hands. I backed off toward the exit, murmuring, "Thank, thank you very much, I really appreciate it."

On the street, in the autumn slush, I took a deep breath, did two pirou- ettes, and launched myself on the alluring path to Paris.

"Tolya," I said to my husband later that day, "I need a notarized state- ment from you that you don't object to my visiting Paris."

"Good God, why should I object?"

"OVIR wants to know that you're giving me permission to go to Paris while in sound mind and not under hypnosis or the influence of drugs and alcohol. That's in Form No. 6."

"Oh, I see," said Tolya respectfully. "Tomorrow I'll take a day off and drop by the Notary Public. Do I need a note from a psychiatrist?"

"You don't, but I will, for sure. And from a dozen other doctors as well."

"Right! And don't forget to drop by the coroner's office. His autopsy re- port might well be the deciding factor."

In the morning, I raced over to the Apartment Management Office. Naturally, they were not receiving that day, but I found a friendly clerk who, in exchange for a pair of imported pantyhose, filled out Form No. 86 regarding the number of people in my family whom I would be leaving be- hind as hostages. By evening, I had in my possession two documents. In- spired by this initial success, I bought a folder, wrote "France" on it with a red pencil, and thus laid the groundwork for my Paris trip.

My next step was an assault on the Outpatient Clinic. Rushing from re- ceptionist to receptionist, I finagled passes that got me doctors' appoint- ments ahead of the waiting line. My organism was studied by an orthope- dist and an internist, urologist, and neurologist. I choked on a rubber tube and swallowed barium. I hastened down crowded corridors, carrying con- tainers with wastes of my internal organs. I stood in front of and lay down under powerful X-ray equipment. They even stuck a red light into my rear, which made me look like the latest model of the Toyota hatchback. Two weeks later, the doctors decided unanimously that as far as my internal or- gans were concerned, I was fit. One detail remained—the Head Doctor's signature. He raised his pen, but suddenly it froze in the air.

"Where is the release from the Venereal Disease Clinic? I don't see their signature."

"Are you kidding . . . Are you suggesting . . ." I began on a high note but was interrupted by a mercilessly logical question: "Why should we take your word for it?" There was no answer, and I retreated.

The Regional V.D. Clinic worked on a first come–first served basis. I had to wait more than two hours before a lady doctor called my name. Her face was severe and gloomy, without a glimmer of a friendly smile.

"Would you sign this paper, please? It's for going abroad."

"What do you mean, 'Sign this?'" she said dryly. I don't sign anything just like that. You'll need to have a blood test here; you will know the results in three days."

"Blood test? For what?"

"Gonorrhea, for one."

"Maybe syphilis?"

"That's always a possibility," nodded the doctor.

"This is ridiculous . . . Simply absurd! You make me laugh!"

"I advise you not to be too quick to laugh. If you, by any chance, turn out to be healthy, then laugh all you want."

By that time my optimism had evaporated without a trace. I walked out of the doctor's office on wooden legs and, accompanied by compassionate looks from a bunch of young men, dragged myself to the entrance hall. In the mirror, my face was the color of chopped liver with a purple crater for a nose.

But my luck held. Three days later I got my precious certificate, which declared that Comrade Dargis was clear of all the sexually transmittable diseases listed on the form.

"You may be fine physically, but what about your Soviet morals? Do you think you will pass?" asked my husband.

The question was far from frivolous. My political attitude had to be approved by my boss, by the chairman of the local Union, and by the Regional Communist Party Committee.

"Now, who would write me a recommendation for going abroad?" I appealed to Comrade Pypin.

"Run over to the Trade Union Committee. The girls there have the right forms."

The secretary raised her blue Botticelli-like eyes. "Which form do you want? To be released on bail or to get on the list for a co-op apartment?"

"No, I need the form for going abroad."

"To a socialist or a capitalist country?"

"Capitalist country."

She provided me with a form, the last line of which read: "The Administration, Party Committee, and Trade Union Committee recommend Comrade [blank] for a trip to [blank] and bear full responsibility for this recommendation."

In the corridor I read the entire text of the recommendation. Had I possessed all the virtues listed therein, I could have easily qualified for the Supreme Court, or to have my ashes buried in a funerary urn in the Kremlin wall.

Once I had all my papers stamped and signed, I had to present myself to the Regional Party Committee. A schoolmate of mine, the then-head of the Department of Marxist Philosophy at the university, brought me a ton of Party propaganda. Inspired by a glass of Armenian cognac, he briefed me on the significance of the Communist Party Congresses. Finally, I gulped down a Valium and set out for the interview, whispering to myself the names of the Communist leaders of the numerous Communist countries and the names of the heads of nations belonging to NATO.

The Regional Party Committee was housed in the former mansion of Count Gagarin. Marble cupids aimed their arrows at me; crystal chandeliers glimmered with blue and rose sparkles; the stairway was covered with a scarlet carpet. Lenin's plaster bust was framed by rare tropical plants, as was becoming for the Founder of the First Socialist Country in the World.

About a dozen people were in the waiting room. An architect who had been invited to erect something grandiose in Morocco was nervously writing on a note pad. Two professors on their way to temporarily friendly Ghana were flipping through *Party Life* magazine. A quartet of musicians—heralds of Soviet culture to Finland—chirped by the window.

One by one these people disappeared behind the massive oak door. When they reappeared their crimson faces, which looked as if they had just come out of a high-pressure cooker, revealed nothing about whether or not they had been granted permission to go abroad.

Finally it was my turn. Thirteen members of the Regional Party Committee sat around the table with an air of great importance. I perched modestly on the edge of a chair.

"This comrade has received an invitation from France to visit her uncle," Guzin, the secretary began. "Are there any questions for the comrade?"

"How is your uncle related to you?" asked a rotund lady without a neck.

"He is my uncle," I answered firmly.

"Could you specify in what sense?"

"In the sense that he is my mother's brother."

"Interesting. How did your uncle end up in France?" The sounds came from somewhere to the side.

"His parents moved there when he was a child." Twenty-six eyes looked at me reproachfully.

"At what age?" Guzin asked severely.

"At two," I said, taking three years off my uncle's age at the time, hoping it would mitigate his criminal act.

"And when did this occur?"

"In 1913 . . . four years before the Revolution." I moved even further back in time.

"So why go see him if you don't even know him?"

"I do know him; he visited the U.S.S.R."

"Then why go see him if you have already seen him?"

Why indeed? I didn't have a single convincing argument in my head.

"Hum . . . I want to meet his family and . . . see France."

"So you've seen everything in your own country? Have you visited Siberia, for example?" an old man representing the Committee of Retired People put in nastily.

"Not yet," I responded meekly, "but you see, my uncle isn't there."

"Have you visited a capitalist country before?" asked someone skinny and jaundiced.

"This will be the first time."

"There, you see . . ." he exulted, baring his yellow teeth. "You've got no experience traveling in capitalist countries. It is dangerous. Better start with a socialist country, say, for example, Bulgaria."

"In principle, you are absolutely right, but my uncle happens to live in France."

"Under what auspices did he visit the Soviet Union? If it's not confidential?"

"He is a movie director. He was shooting a documentary film here."

"Is he famous?" The lady without a neck looked jealous.

"I should say so!" I said proudly, "And almost a Marxist."

"How exciting! Does he happen to know Yves Montand?"

I was about to tell her that he was a sort of uncle to Montand, too, but just then Comrade Guzin snorted at the lady and pronounced: "Your family circumstances are clear. But are you aware of the economic and political situation in France?"

"I think so."

"Don't forget that all Soviet people will be judged by your knowledge and behavior. Do you understand your responsibility?"

After this question, the inquisitors knitted their brows and got down to business. I realized that now, after the overture, the real show was about to begin.

"What is the Party makeup in the French coalition government?"

"What is the comparative production of steel, oil, and electric energy in the U.S.A., England, France, and the Benelux countries?"

"Why?" "What for?" "Which?" The questions poured out like peas from an overly ripe pod. I felt like a fly beating frantically against a window, trying to dodge the blows of a dish towel. When I answered questions about puppet governments in Latin America and the military operations in the Parrot's Beak and the Fishhook, I felt on the verge of cardiac arrest. Blackness floated before my eyes; my ears popped as they do in an airplane.

"Are you aware that Nixon personally visited the American Sixth Fleet?" The words sounded as if they were coming from a closet. "Your comments?"

"Yankee, go home! Get out of our Soviet Mediterranean!" I wanted to howl, but restrained myself.

Silence followed. Outside, through the windows, the street lights illuminated the embankment. Guzin glanced at his watch and shot out, "Well, then, do we approve the comrade's application?"

He was in a hurry to get home because in half an hour the U.S.S.R.–Czechoslovakia hockey match was starting on television. The Committee voted yes, and I reeled down the stairs, all but sliding into the tropical plants over Lenin's bust.

The next morning, I conveyed my fat folder labeled "France" to OVIR.

"You managed that very quickly," grinned Kabashkin.

Brazenly, I said, "I hope that my application will not be held up here."

"I don't make any decisions. I am only a clerk. But meanwhile, get ready. Don't waste time."

I did not waste a moment. As a gift to my uncle, I spent a month's salary on a two-pound can of black caviar.

"If they don't let you out, we'll enjoy the caviar ourselves," suggested my compassionate husband.

Meanwhile, friends kept calling, asking me to get various things for them in France. In exchange, they offered me hand-made woolen shawls from the Ural Mountains, silver holders for tea glasses, dried mushrooms, lace, semiprecious stones, wooden spoons, and folk music instruments, including an oversized nineteenth-century balalaika.

Three months passed. Snow fell and melted. OVIR was as silent as

Lenin's tomb. My heart sank at the thought that Parisian chestnut trees would blossom without me. So I called Kabashkin.

"Unfortunately, there's no answer." He sounded like a velvet cello. "But the minute we get any news, we'll let you know."

Finally, the OVIR called.

Gallant Kabashkin offered me a chair and an ashtray.

"I must inform you," his copper basin face glowed, "that your trip to France has been turned down. Your documents will remain with us," said he, patting the folder tenderly.

"Why?" I bellowed with all the air in my lungs.

"That's the way it is. If you wish to apply again, you will have to fill out new forms."

"But why was I turned down?"

"Your uncle is not considered to be a sufficiently close relative to justify the visit."

"What should I do?"

"The rules allow you to apply again a year from now," Kabashkin said, shrugging his shoulders.

"But a year from now our relationship will not have gotten any closer!" I exploded.

"That's logical," Kabashkin perked up. "Quite logical, indeed."

"But what should I write to my uncle? How can I explain? He won't understand a bizarre reason like that."

"Why should he? He doesn't have to know. Write him that you're swamped with work, that you're on the brink of a scientific discovery, that you're sick . . ." He offered the usual excuses.

"I'm sick? With what?" I suddenly heard myself crying. "What illness do I have? Swollen glands? Cancer? Syphilis?"

Kabashkin's face darkened. He went round the table and opened the door for me. I ended up in the reception room. Behind my back his caressing voice murmured to the secretary: "Next, please."

5 Golden Childhood

Biographies of Soviet writers, artists, or composers often begin in this way: "The parents of little Sasha [or Misha or Grisha] were progressive and educated people. Young Sasha [or Misha or Grisha] grew up in an atmosphere of love and devotion to the arts. Literary soirees and concerts were often held at home, skits were put on, fascinating philosophical debates took place . . ."

All of that would have applied to my family had I been born a hundred or even thirty-seven years earlier. But I was born at the end of the 1930s, the years of the most severe Stalinist terror. Everyone who might have been visiting us in our cozy living room was languishing in prison camps instead. Those who were not imprisoned did not visit each other and did not get involved in public philosophical debates. Even when they bumped into each other on the streets, writers, artists, and composers were afraid to acknowledge each other. You never knew which one of them might possibly turn out to be a snitch or a KGB informer.

When my father celebrated his birthday in 1956, which was after Stalin's death, the remnants of the old intellectual elite gathered at our table. Not one of them had avoided the hell of Stalinist repression.

My father's was one of the most interesting cases. He was a law professor and taught at Leningrad University before World War II. Because of a congenital heart defect, he was not drafted, although he tried to volunteer for the front on the very first day of the war. At that time he also worked at the Leningrad Public Library, where he received an assignment to hide and save the rare books and priceless manuscripts.

One morning in 1941, four months after Germany invaded the Soviet Union, my father came down to the library cafeteria to have a cup of boiling water, which was all the cafeteria had to offer. There he met Valya, a waitress whom he had known since she was a child. After school she used to come to this very place with her mother, also a waitress, and do her home work. When her mother died from cancer, Valya replaced her at work. She was friendly and cheerful, and everybody loved her.

Apart from Valya, there was only one other person there, the historian Faina Drobman, a very old friend of my father. He respected her profound knowledge and loved her kind and good nature.

Valya poured hot water into two cups, and at the very same minute the radio transmitted a new report from the front: "THE SOVIET ARMY HAS RE-TREATED FROM THE TOWN OF OREL. THE TOWN IS IN FASCIST HANDS."

"Good Lord," my father said. "Instead of hugging and kissing with Hitler and von Ribbentrop, they should have been strengthening the country's defense potential."

The next morning, a Black Raven came for my father at the Public Library, and he was transported from his Rare Books Department to KGB headquarters. My father spent the first winter of the Leningrad Siege in the KGB internal prison, known as the Big House. He was accused of anti-Soviet and pro-German propaganda. He was under interrogation for more than eleven months. The interrogator beat him with a thick volume of Marx's *Das Kapital* for lack of anything heavier.

By sheer luck my father survived that winter. It was only thanks to our former nanny, Nulya, who worked at the Leningrad military hospital, where one of her duties was to clean the apartment of the hospital head, Colonel Maltsev, and to look after his spaniel, Roy.

Maltsev, an old bachelor, hypochondriac, and misanthrope, adored his dog and fed it condensed milk. Nulya carried the remains of the dog's meals to Father in the Big House. The milk was confiscated by his interrogator, naturally, who saw to it that my father did not die from starvation or the beatings. After all, if he had, the food donations would have stopped.

Fortunately, my father's file came to the attention of a military prosecutor who had graduated from Leningrad University three years before the war began, and who was one of my father's best pupils. There was no trial, and the prosecutor's signature was enough to free my father. By that time he was on the verge of dying from starvation and had to be hospitalized immediately.

My father-in-law was less fortunate: he died of hunger at the age of thirty-four during the Leningrad Siege, as did the young waitress Valya. As for Faina Drobman, the other person who was in the cafeteria on that fatal morning, she survived the war. We met her on the street five years later. She was bent over with arthritis and could hardly walk. Her entire family had perished in the war, and she was absolutely alone. We visited her from time to time, always taking her some groceries.

"Pa, tell me, isn't it possible, that Faina squealed?" I asked for the hundredth time.

"No, out of the question." He stubbornly shook his head.

"So that means Valya did?"

"It's absolutely impossible. I remember her as a little girl."

"And yet it was one of them."

"Possibly," Father would admit reluctantly. "But I prefer to live and die in ignorance."

Meanwhile Mother and I were in the town of Molotov in the Ural Mountains, to which the children's boarding school of the Writers Union had been evacuated. In Molotov, the Leningraders were housed in a seven-story hotel under the same roof as a rather posh group from the Kirov Opera and Ballet Theater, the Ballet School, and the Writers Union. In the brick building on Karl Marx Street that housed the local theater, the Kirov company began a four-year engagement, the longest in its history. There I received what biographies usually describe as a "brilliant musical education": evacuee children were allowed to be present during rehearsals.

At the tender age of four, my friend Natasha Levina and I did not miss out on this opportunity. Every morning at nine o'clock we stood by the locked theater entrance. The watchman, Gargonych, was the first to appear. Smoking a hand-rolled cigarette, he opened the door, asked us about events on the Leningrad Front, and let us into the unheated hall. "You just sit still like mice, or I'll sweep you out with my broom."

I listened to Tchaikovsky's *Queen of Spades* forty-two times and to *Eugene Onegin* fifty-seven, except for scene two of the second act. At the question "Where, where, oh, where have you gone, the golden days of my spring?" my nose would begin to twitch in anticipation of an inevitable tragedy. During the scene of the duel when Onegin and Lensky sang their duet, "Should we turn it into a joke while our hands are yet unstained by blood? Should we part as friends?" my nerves broke down. I rushed out of the auditorium and hid in the bathroom. The sound of the shots of the fatal duel did not reach that far. Several minutes later I would return, opening the door a crack and whispering, "Have they made up?"

Natasha would sadly shake her head, "They wouldn't even think of it." I still held on to the hope that tomorrow Onegin would take pity on Lensky, who would marry Olga, and Tatyana would leave her general for Onegin. As we all know, this has yet to happen. So I have never seen the duel scene.

I was not, however, a bit frightened by the scene in the *Queen of Spades* in which the ghost of a dead countess comes into the barracks. A lack of funds for lighting prevented a proper presentation of a quivering, hazy apparition. The ghost of the Queen of Spades entered the barracks dressed in some dirty gray rags. She was not frightening at all, and I could not for the life of me comprehend why Hermann retreated from her in horror.

"Sergei, my dear boy, don't be so zealous," the director shouted into the megaphone. "Stand by the sofa and just lean against the armrest." But Hermann never listened to his advice and, with a dismissive wave of his hand, flung himself onto the sofa. The upholstery would invariably snap, letting out clouds of dust, and the springs either threw Hermann up in the air or stuck in his behind. The props just could not hold up under such passion.

Academician Joseph Orbeli, a close friend of my parents, taught me to love and understand painting. He was then the director of the Hermitage museum, while his wife, Antonina Izergina, curated the European art section.

After closing time in the evening or on Thursdays, when the Hermitage was closed to the public, Orbeli would take his son, Mitya, and me around the empty regal halls of the Hermitage. I knew inside out the collection of Impressionists kept in the storeroom, and I even combed my hair with the famous gold Scythian combs. Sometimes we sat in the Gold Room while Orbeli read us excerpts from his favorite Armenian epic, *David of Sasun,* which left three-year-old Mitya quite cold. He would slide from his father's lap and furiously spin around like a puppy in pursuit of its tail.

"I'll get you!" Orbeli thundered. He grabbed Mitya by the hand, pressed him to his chest, and stroked him until Mitya buried his nose into his father's beard and fell asleep.

Mitya was the only child of Orbeli. He was born with a complicated congenital heart defect when Orbeli was fifty-nine. The doctors predicted a short life for him: Mitya would not make it to his fifth, seventh, twelfth birthdays. The family, in constant fear of Mitya's illness, lived under this sword of

Damocles. "I pray to God every day," his mother, Totya, would say, "that Orbeli and I do not live to that day, that the Lord may take us sooner."

Fate was kind to this family, as it turned out. Mitya outlived his parents. He died at the age of twenty-five, a graduate student at the Institute of Cytology.

The director of the Leningrad Public Library, Lev Rakov, an extremely handsome man and one of the most brilliant minds among my parents' friends, introduced me to the world of books. Rakov joked that his real calling was to be a prisoner. The first time, he was jailed in 1937 in connection with the case of Professor Kovalev, a historian of ancient Rome, who was accused of digging a tunnel from the history department building on Vasilevsky Island to the Palace Square. Under torture he named accomplices, including Lev Rakov. Rakov was released in 1941. He volunteered for the front and finished the war in the rank of colonel.

He was jailed for the second time in 1949, when he was director of the Museum of Leningrad Siege; that time for allegedly hiding weapons in museum exhibits. He was sentenced to seven years in prison camps and returned to Leningrad one spring morning in 1956. His wife, Marina, herself having recently returned from exile in Kazakhstan, called us that morning: "Lev is coming home today!"

To this day I can still hear her ringing voice. She and my mother rushed from one shop to another and managed to buy an entire wardrobe: a suit, a shirt, a tie, boots, and even a handkerchief for the breast pocket. We decided that Marina would bring him to our home straight from the train station, for there was no bathtub in their communal apartment. Having persuaded our neighbors to put off doing their laundry until the next day, we heated up the gas stove in the bathroom. Meanwhile, Nulya cooked mushroom soup and some savory hamburgers.

The bell rang at seven in the evening. Lev Rakov stood in the doorway dressed in his prison quilted jacket and heavy boots. He was haggard and unshaven, and he had a bluish scar across his cheek. "Greetings, dear friends, but I won't shake hands with you because I am filthy and disgusting." Without taking off his jacket, he proceeded straight to the bathroom. He spent a whole hour splashing in the water and emerged elegant, fragrant, yet monstrously aged. Sitting at the table sideways, he drank a glass of vodka, glancing briefly at the hissing frying pan full of hamburgers. Suddenly dropping his head on the table, he began to sob loudly and uncontrollably.

*   *   *

A young man by the name of George Vellet, the son of a French Commu-
nist, who immigrated to Russia after the war to seek happiness in the land
of the Soviets, tutored me in French. George studied at the Institute of
Foreign Languages and earned some extra money by giving private lessons.
For all the years that he taught me French we struggled through Victor
Hugo's *Les Miserables*. The lessons always began with the question "Jean
Valjean, *etait-il pauvre ou riche?*"

"Huh?" was my intelligent response. I couldn't care less about Jean
Valjean.

My thoughts were occupied with my faithful admirers Billy Goat, Mammoth, and Airplane, who used to wait for me at the front entrance after
school. Romantic pursuits in my childhood were carried out in the following manner. Nulya would dispatch me to get some bread or kerosene. De-
scending the stairs with a shopping bag or a large can, I would invariably
find the three figures in cowboy jackets and "Cockney caps" waiting for me.
They would detach themselves from the wall and silently follow me at a distance of three or four steps, standing guard by the door of the bakery or
kerosene shop and then escorting me back home in the same manner. I pretended not to notice them, but as I passed the neighbor girls playing jacks
or hopscotch in the yard I could not repress a triumphant grin.

At some later point Billy Goat revealed his feelings for me. During a spring
cleaning session his mother told him to take out some trash. Billy Goat was
too lazy to walk down the four flights of steps, so he threw the junk right
out of the window. We circled below hoping to catch something valuable
as Billy Goat distributed the trophies from above. He leaned out holding
two dusty paper roses in his hands. We waited with bated breath.

"For Tanya," he bellowed. "If anyone else touches them I'll break some
arms!"

Once Billy Goat and Airplane robbed the second-hand clothes dealer
Yefim Magid. We heard strange noises in the middle of the night. My father hastened into the hallway in his underwear and turned on the light.
The front door banged shut, and someone fell head over heels down the
stairs. Father saw a suitcase crammed with lengths of cloth, clocks, gold
rings, and table silverware. On the suitcase was a note, "To our dear Tanya
from Two Musketeers." Both musketeers soon found themselves in a home
for juvenile delinquents and disappeared from my life forever. A pioneer of

free enterprise, Yefim Magid did not survive in the framework of the Socialist system and also did time at some point.

As for Mammoth, his family lived in the building across the way. Either our curtains were too transparent or I forgot to draw them; in any case, Mammoth somehow glimpsed the most intimate part of my life. My nanny, Nulya, who was very religious, would not let me go to bed without having said my prayers. My parents had nothing against religion, but they insisted that no icons hang in my room—why give anyone yet another reason to snitch? Every evening Nulya came into my room, placed an icon of St. Nicholas on my desk, and made me pray on my knees. I had to repeat "Our Father," "Lord in Heaven," and "The Virgin Maiden Rejoice" three times.

Mammoth must have seen me pray and snitched on me at school. At a school meeting, the Young Pioneer leader gave an atheistic speech, concluding that I presented a threat to the entire Young Pioneer Organization, was corrupting the minds of my comrades, and should be thrown out of their ranks. I was banned from the Pioneers while Mammoth was given a certificate for vigilance. At home, humiliated and inconsolable, I burst into tears, burying my face against Nulya's knees. Nulya dashed straight over to Mammoth's father to give him a piece of her mind.

Mammoth Senior was a one-legged war veteran, a shoemaker in peacetime. Every night he shut the basement window on which a sign read "Shoe Repair" and hobbled to the nearby grocery store for a bottle of red-pepper vodka. After drinking himself into a frenzy he would unfasten his artificial leg and beat his wife and son with it. Screams and curses could be heard from their apartment until two in the morning.

An hour after Nulya's visit our doorbell rang. On the landing stood Mammoth-the-father holding Mammoth-the-son by the ear.

"Is your Tanya at home?" the elder Mammoth asked. "Have her come here."

I stepped out cautiously into the hallway. Neighbors stuck out their heads from behind doors cracked open. When he saw me, the shoemaker slapped his son in the face and kicked him with such force that Mammoth crashed at my feet like an empty sack.

"Beg her forgiveness, you no-good piece of shit! Loud and clear, so that we can all hear you! Rat on someone again and I'll kill you, scum! Pioneer, my ass!"

I was not reinstated in the Pioneers, but three years later I joined the

Komsomol, though not for long because my passion for defending "the in-sulted and the injured" often got me into trouble.

One of the most pitiful figures in our class was Sarah Mezericher. To live with such an obviously Jewish name in the Soviet Union was not at all easy, especially if you had a hooked nose, black wiry hair, and a thick head to boot. Sarah's predicament was exacerbated by the fact that her father, Sam-uel, had a new wife, Klava, an ethnic Russian who had two sons from her first marriage. All five of them lived in one room. Klava, a huge woman with beady, cold eyes and a wide backside, worked at a railway station snack bar. She gulped down her first glass of vodka and a fish sandwich at ten in the morning. By seven in the evening her face was crimson, and a destruc-tive rage was burning inside her. Her sixteen-year-old twins, Albert and Edward, got drunk in other parts of the city. Unless they spent their energy in some street fight on the way home, they would let off steam once they arrived, turning the household into a scene of fierce ethnic conflict.

The three ethnic Russians would attack the two Jews. Samuel—tiny and frail, with a heavy pelican nose—and clumsy Sarah heroically defended their corner of the room. But if Sarah got a poor mark at school, Samuel and Klava joined their forces to give her a dressing-down. In the eighth grade when Sarah received an end-of-term C in history, she buried her face in her arms and sobbed bitterly.

"What is the meaning of these theatrics?" the history teacher, Serafima Yegorovna, asked in an icy tone. She assumed a Napoleonic posture with her arms crossed over her chest, leaning against the world map.

"Please, Serafima Yegorovna, give Mezericher a B," I pleaded. "Sarah's stepmother beats her when she gets a C."

"Obviously, not enough. She hasn't beaten her laziness out of her."

"Serafima Yegorovna, in the name of the whole class, I beg you, change the grade."

"How dare you pester me like this! I have no patience for you kids! First you twiddle your thumbs the whole year, and then you whine about the re-sults. As the saying goes, Moscow doesn't believe in tears."

"Oh, but please change it, just this once."

"Enough of this nonsense! This is not a charity ward! To obtain a higher grade in such a manner is a disgrace. If I were you I would burn with shame!"

"But, Serafima Yegorovna, the end justifies the means."

"Well, well! And just where did you learn such wisdom?"

"Many historical and political figures think so."

"Who, for example?"

Sarah Mezericher was forgotten. The class held their breath as they watched our duel. The history teacher's face turned stone-cold, and her jaw stuck out like a car ashtray.

"For example, Frederick Nietzsche . . ." I felt myself sinking fast, but I could not stop.

"How fascinating. Have you actually read his works?"

"Of course. *Beyond Good and Evil* and *Thus Spake Zarathustra*."

"Perhaps you read some of Hitler's works as well?"

"Perhaps."

Serafima peeled herself off the world map.

"Stay in your seats until the bell rings." Bowing her head, she quickly walked out of the classroom.

Who was more frightened? I, who said it, or she, who heard it? The bell had not finished ringing when Zoya Vasilyevna, our classroom teacher, walked in. She was permanently pregnant and had pigment stains on her puffy face.

"Now you've done it, Verkhovskaya. Go home immediately and bring back your parents. Straight to the principal's office. You have just been thrown out off the Komsomol; now you're going to be expelled from school."

It was 1952. Two months previously Father had lost his job at the Library of the Academy of Sciences and now was slowly recovering from a heart attack. I simply could not deliver him yet another blow. What should I do? Should I talk to the principal myself? The principal was a fearsome figure, exuding a kind of solemn, funereal chill. In all my years at school I was in her office only three times.

I knocked on her door.

"Come in." She rose up from behind her desk and fixed me with her tin-plated eyes.

"I did not invite you."

"May I please speak to you, Galina Mefodeevna?"

"I have nothing to discuss with you. Other comrades will speak to both you and your parents in precisely one hour. Now, get out!"

No one was at home. I wandered around our communal apartment, knocking on various doors. Nobody was in. Our neighbors Nahum and

Faina Borenboyms' door was unlocked. Faina had always been sickly, and I had often noticed heaps of pills on her dresser. I did not know the names of any poisons except for potassium cyanide, which of course she did not keep. But sifting through the packets and bottles I ran across some ampoules labeled "morphine moriartic." *"Mourir"* in French means "to die" — just what I needed. I broke open the thin glass necks and drank the contents of both ampoules. Then I put our husky, Jack, on a leash and took him out for a walk. For some reason I did not want my death to take place at home.

It began to rain. I let go of the leash, and Jack raced after a stray cat. Leaning against a wet stack of firewood, I stood still and waited. There was not a soul around. Jack drove the cat out of its territory, sat down in a puddle, and lifted his light-gray eyes at me as if to say, "What are we waiting for?" As I reached down to pet him, suddenly the yard began to sway, the stack of wood fell off to the left, the damp windows of the buildings rushed to the right, and the last thing I heard was the dog's piercing yelp.

I regained consciousness in a hospital bed, my stomach having been pumped and cleaned with oceans of water. Perhaps that morphine had been prepared as *moriartic,* but it must have been so old that its lethal properties had evaporated long ago. I had poisoned myself with an expired drug. Faced with this suicide attempt, the frightened school officials and the "other comrades" decided to leave me and my parents alone.

However, my childhood and my adolescence, too, ended with that episode.

6 Mentors

Among the succession of teachers who have passed through my life like dim memories, I remember two whose striking personalities aroused in me at the time feelings of hatred and contempt. Now, many years later, even though I have long since seen the last of them, I cannot help but feel sorrow and shame.

Visions of my math teacher Maria Grigoryevna still haunt my dreams at night. She had thin, gray hair, which she wore in a small bun on the crown of her head, and a sunken, toothless mouth. Perched on the end of her nose were iron-rimmed glasses with one cracked lens and a string around her head to hold them in place. She wore a shabby dark-blue suit, coarse stockings, and huge men's boots.

In one hand Maria Grigoryevna carried a string bag full of copybooks and in the other a T-square with which she banged us on the head. Her strikes were as quick as lightning, not intended so much for pain as for humiliation. She also had an unbearable nasal twang and a biting sense of humor.

"Well now, let us begin the Slaughter of the Innocent," she would challenge the class as she burst into the classroom with her T-square, like a tank with its gun turret aimed at us. "Verkhovskaya, Ruchkina, Kozina, Petrova, and Sherer . . . to the board!"

"There's not enough room at the board for the five of us," a plaintive voice cried out.

Maria Grigoryevna grinned like a toothless Cheshire cat. "Considering how much you know, there is more than enough room." Having taken her sadistic pleasure in our failure to solve the problems or prove the theorems, she sat back in a more comfortable position and began the vivisection: "So, let's start with Verkhovskaya [that's me]. Practically brainless, a degenerate to the core. Just like my son. In algebra he doesn't know x from y; in geometry he's even worse. I tell him: 'Shame on you, monster, where are your mathematical genes? Your father was practically Pythagoras, and I am no idiot.' And do you know what that good-for-nothing piece of shit says? 'Those genes are still dormant, Mom, but don't worry. Homer was no math whiz either.'"

"So, your son is a talented poet?" I ventured.

"Yes, indeed," she drew a crumpled piece of paper out of her pocket. "Listen to this, I stole it from his desk:

> And my heart yearns for human kindness,
> But I have no friends and nobody to love,
> As if I am condemned
> To loneliness eternal.

"Note that my chickadee complains about loneliness, even after I bought him a pair of galoshes at the flea market. True, one turned out to be a half inch longer than the other, but with a little newspaper stuffed in it . . ." Suddenly, she remembered I was there.

"Say, how are things up there on the Western Front?"

On the "Western Front" things looked pretty grim.

"What a shame, Verkhovskaya. You get an F, but even an F is too high a grade for you. And don't forget to show your report card to your father rather than to your overprotective mom."

"Where did you get the idea that my mom is overprotective? She never defends me."

"Really? Let me then tell you a little story. Don't interrupt, and don't try to deny it. Last quarter you whistled in the classroom's closet, right? You slid down the banister, didn't you? What did you do with the eggs that were given to you for experiments in chemistry? You fried them sunny side up. In gym class you feigned an epileptic fit. I cannot recall all of your dirty tricks, but in two weeks you had eleven demerits in your assignment notebook, all of them signed by your mother—or so your classroom teacher, the naive Zoya Vasilyevna, thought. I said to her: 'Call her parents. The girl is going downhill.' But she says to me: 'The parents know. After all, they've been signing her assignment notebook.' Then I summoned your mother myself . . . Shall I go on?"

"That won't be necessary, Maria Grigoryevna . . . please."

Naturally, my parents had no idea about what was going on. I signed the assignment notebook myself, forging my mother's name. I remembered the day when my mother and I had walked into the teachers' room, which had been empty except for the hag math teacher.

"Why aren't you paying any attention to the child," she asked as she thrust the notebook under my mother's nose. "Why do you not react? At this rate, she will grow up a criminal."

Mama stared at the demerits next to "her" signatures, then looked at me.

"Have you been really signing these?" Maria Grigoryevna asked.

A moment's pause, as Mama caught her breath.

"Yes, I signed them. Excuse me, Maria Grigoryevna, for having taken no action so far. I promise to have a very serious talk with Tanya. I hope that she will no longer give us cause for such grief."

When we went out into the hallway Mama broke into tears. "I am so ashamed that my daughter has turned into such a shallow, cowardly, no good . . ."

The last thing I wanted was to hear this story again.

"Sit down, Verkhovskaya, I'm tired of looking at you." Maria Grigoryevna turned her attention to her next victim at the blackboard. "So, now we move on to Kozina, to our little nun. By the way, where did you do your homework yesterday?"

"At home, where else . . ." Kozina spoke in her contralto voice.

"Oh, really? That means I mistook you for somebody else. You see, I was walking home from Party headquarters last night. The moon was shining, the stars were sparkling. And suddenly what did I see but Kozina in the embrace of a handsome young man. On Kozina's head was a divine hat. Not a hat but a cream puff. 'Oh,' I said to myself, 'my life is practically over, and when have I ever had such a hat? And when have I ever been in Apollo's embrace?' And I answered, 'Never!'"

"It was not a young man at all," Kozina persisted. "It was my father."

"No kidding?" A shocked Maria Grigoryevna slumped back in her chair. "Your father, you say? He has preserved himself remarkably well; one would not think he had more than eighteen years on him. Sit, my little one, and ask your handsome daddy to go over your homework. In the meantime, you get a solid D! Well now, how is Petrova doing? Petrova is doing . . . quite poorly! Oh, you miserable creature! That is not a brain in your head but pea soup. Still, I know you have worked very hard. What will you be doing after graduation? Not anything in the field of mathematics, I hope?"

"N-no, I will go to veterinary . . ."

Maria Grigoryevna nodded approvingly.

"To cure animals is a noble occupation. Just for that I am giving you a B, just for your noble soul. But do me a personal favor—don't go anywhere near mathematics. It will kill you. Now! Just look at Sherer, our home-grown Einstein. I can see sparks of intelligence and glimmers of thought here."

Maria Grigoryevna walked up to the board and examined Sherer's scribbles attentively.

"You have a talent, my girl, but don't get excited too soon! Though I am tempted to give you an A, I will not. I will instead call upon you again tomorrow, just to make sure."

Only Ruchkina was left at the board, and Maria Grigoryevna, looking at her chalk-stained nose, sorrowfully shook her head.

"Shame on you! You, who live in a single-family apartment, and your father is a lawyer. You should have been an 'A' student. You probably even eat apples every day."

Confessing to "eating apples," Ruchkina, in tears, tugged at her skirt.

"I will give you a 'C' for a change, because I am tired of this three-ring circus. But let me tell you all, this is not a classroom but a Museum of Natural Freaks. Sit down."

Good Lord! How we were frightened of her, and how we hated the malicious old woman, although she was probably a good teacher—no one failed math at the university entrance exams. But at the time we neither knew nor cared about her personal life, nor about what a horrible hand she had been dealt.

Maria Grigoryevna was then only forty-seven years old. Her husband had been killed at the front. She was cooped up in one room with her paralyzed mother, her son, and twin girls, the daughters of a friend who had died during the siege of Leningrad. She supported this whole mob on her pitiful teacher's salary. In 1956, during the Soviet invasion of Hungary, her son, then a University student of philology, read his poem at the Komsomol meeting:

The Russian octopus,
The Russian Big Brother,
Swallowing Budapest.
The Soviet tanks
Rolled over the city
And drowned its beauty in blood.

Needless to say, the very next day he was arrested while Maria Grigoryevna was fired from her job and lost her teaching license.

Frieda Naumovna, our French teacher, was the most miserable and contemptible creature in the entire school. She wore a stained yet fancy-looking blouse and had pudgy cheeks and a nose so overpowdered it looked frostbitten. She edged into the classroom sideways, her eyes timorously scanning the room in anticipation of the next prank. *"Bonjour, mes enfans,"* she quietly said into thin air as the class buzzed and shook violently. *"Les enfants"* ignored her presence. Frieda coughed hoarsely, trying to attract attention.

Desk tops banged, paper birds flew above our heads in all directions, Nadya Kopteva danced a fandango on the windowsill, and in the closet somebody rattled a mop and howled. We were taking revenge for the humiliation we had suffered in math class. Frieda tried every tactic she could think of. First she appealed to our compassion: "Children, do you hear, I have completely lost my voice and cannot outshout you. I have a sore throat. It hurts me to raise my voice. Please, I beg of you: calm down!"

The class refused to acknowledge her presence. Taking a deep breath, she changed her tactics. This time she tried a combination of flattery and bragging. "How young and charming you all are. I look at you, and it warms my heart. What vitality! Of course, you cannot imagine that I was once just like that. One day the Tzar himself visited our school with his daughters, grand dukes, guards, and other very high-ranking officials. We were gathered in the Blue Hall, and when His Majesty entered, music sounded, and all of us—in white dresses—bowed down in a deep curtsey, just like white swans!" Frieda lifted her crooked, arthritic finger. "You see, young ladies, how well we were brought up!"

"Which Tzar was that? Peter the Great, or what?"

"Comment donc? Of course not! *C'etait notre dernier l'empereur* Nicholas II." Her cheeks blushed from the memory. "And then His Majesty

walked along the rows, stopped in front of me, and said tenderly: *'Elle est charmante! Comment-allez vous, mademoiselle?'"*

The class went on grunting, barking, and hooting. Frieda's encounter with the Romanov family made no impression on us. Frieda made one last attempt. "You must be bored with the grammar, dear friends. You probably have not felt all the beauty of the French language. It is true that the grammar is difficult, but just listen to what divine poetry has been written in French . . ." And the poor thing in her cracked voice solemnly recited Sully-Prudhomme, Rimbaud, Baudelaire, and Verlaine:

> *Je me souviens des jours anciens*
> *Et je pleure . . .*

We would respond with croaking and mooing. Then Frieda would collapse on her chair and, covering her eyes with her hand, begin to sob softly and sorrowfully. Tears would drop from under her small, wrinkled hand right onto the class log book. She would frantically dig into her bag in search of a handkerchief . . . Now I wonder what kind of stone our hearts were made of.

One day, the winter before graduation, when the class for some reason was in a peace-loving mood, Frieda confided to us shyly: "Sometimes we inflict pain on each other, but I cannot get angry. I am very attached to all of you, for aside from you I have no one. I am sure that we will be very sorry to leave each other upon your graduation . . . Don't you think?"

Frieda Naumovna did not live long enough to see us graduate. In early spring she died of throat cancer in the overcrowded cancer ward of the local hospital.

7 Neighbors

For the first twenty years of my life I lived at 32 Dostoyevsky Street. Our family occupied three rooms of a nine-room apartment on the third floor of a beautiful old building. There were Spanish tiles on the stairs, bas-reliefs of flower garlands and exotic birds on the walls, and stained-glass windows. Before the Revolution this apartment belonged to my grandparents. When they and tiny Uncle Paul emigrated to the West, my seventeen-year-old mother stayed there alone. In less than a month, the Bolsheviks took away six of the rooms and converted the apartment into a *kommunalka*, a communal paradise.

Communal apartments are usually the scenes of horror stories, but sometimes they can be places of idyllic calm. Unless everyone sharing the apartment takes up transcendental meditation, this state of calm is attained only through a fortunate chain of events, as was clearly the case with our apartment.

Dostoyevsky Street was famous for the Kuznechny open-air market and the Yamsky public baths. The market disproved the lies of Russia's slanderers about the lack of foodstuffs under Socialism, and the baths had an intriguing reputation as a black market heaven. In the 1960s, it dawned on somebody that Fyodor Dostoyevsky himself had lived across from the market, and a museum devoted to the great writer was opened—with, however, no pomp whatsoever.

Our building competed for the title of the Outstanding-Communist-Way-of-Life-Building, our stairwell vied for the honor of being the Outstanding-Communist-Way-of-Life-Stairwell, and our apartment struggled for the title of the Outstanding-Communist-Way-of-Life-Apartment. Therefore, the parquet floor in the corridor was always shiny, but in the kitchen stood five tables, under five individual dim bulbs, which revealed our communal commitment to the old-fashioned ideas of privacy and independence.

For many years, our apartment kept up a turbulent but trivial life that did not merit any literary attention. But the events of a few days turned our flourishing *kommunalka* into a wasteland. This started with acts of infidelity and ended with a murder in the bathroom.

To the left of the front door lived an engineer from Leningrad Gas, Naum Borenboim, and his wife Faina. Naum was on the stout side, about fifty, moderately bald and moderately roguish. He had light blue, slightly bulging eyes, and his motto was "I love thee, Life!" Faina, though her husband's age, looked like a representative of the previous generation. Gastritis, pancreatitis, and other ailments of the stomach and the intestinal tract had tinted her face greenish-yellow. Her disposition, too, seemed acid with sarcasm.

"That bitch, she only knows snapping or making fun," Senka Roof complained. Senka, a truck driver, lived across the hall from our room. "And besides, she's so underhanded, that over-bleached shrew," added Lily Kuzina, a passport clerk from the Housing Office whose room was to our right.

All of us in the apartment, though, were only innocent bystanders to Faina's sarcastic remarks. The real target was her husband, meek and merry Naum. And everyone could guess why. Naum was engaged in "extracurricular" activities.

He was extremely discrete about his numerous love affairs, and Faina furiously searched for clues, but in vain. She could never find a brassiere in his pocket, or traces of lipstick on his neck, or even a telephone number on a little scrap of paper. Sly Borenboim was crafty and careful. All the same, vibrations of his infidelity somehow resonated in the air.

But one day Naum broke the commandment "Thou shalt not sin too close to home," and God's wrath was unleashed on him. Borenboim let his head be turned by his apartment-mate Lily Kuzina. She was indisputably a real blonde and, despite her bowed legs that could have belonged to a jockey, was a good-looking girl in her thirties.

Lily's personal life flourished when she went on vacation to the Black Sea in the Crimea or the Caucasus. Her love archives preserved memories of sea captains from Murmansk, union officials from Siberia, suppliers from Minsk, and even the chief engineer from a toxic chemicals plant in

Odessa. Of him, Lily observed with endearing warmth, "An old Jew, a bit decrepit, but tender and an easy touch."

Then Lily's practical mind brought her to a realization that there was no need to go to the end of the earth when she could find an old Jew, a bit decrepit, but tender and an easy touch right next door in the persona of Naum Borenboim. So Lily dropped a few hints that Naum would have a chance with her. Flattered, he presented her with a bottle of Kremlin Stars perfume and a sprig of mimosa on International Woman's Day. On two occasions they sneaked off to the movies together. Once Naum asked a friend for the key to his co-op apartment, and he and Lily spent an afternoon there. But for the most part, the romance was kept alive very innocently within the limited space of the communal kitchen, bathroom, and corridor, until something got into them both and they lost their heads.

It was a warm evening in May. Lily was publicly fixing her hair by the mirror in the corridor. Naum buzzed around her under the pretext of using the telephone. Coquettishly blowing some hair from her comb in Borenboim's direction, Lily said: "By the way, tomorrow is my birthday. I'm not inviting anybody over—I've had enough of all that. But my girlfriend has given me a can of crab meat as a present, and we can open it together."

"What can I give you, Lilichka?" Naum asked anxiously.

"You, yourself, Naum dear. I wish that we could spend the day together, just the two of us. I was even hoping that . . ."

"But where and how?" our heated Casanova whispered.

"Well, naturally not in public," Lily said, opening her eyes wide, and Naum went numb with desire. Nevertheless, being a realist, he understood that on such short notice he would never be able to arrange for a place where they could meet.

Then Naum's inflamed brain produced a brilliant strategic plan. He would tell Faina that he was being sent on a business trip for two days, and he would pretend to leave for Moscow in the morning. Faina did not like to be home alone, and, whenever Naum went away, she would stay overnight with her sister. Then Naum would return home in secret and slip into Lily's room, where they would drink cognac, feed on crab meat, and indulge themselves. The next morning, Naum would leave for work and return home that evening "from his trip." This plan was put into action at once.

In the morning Naum "left for Moscow." From that moment, unforeseen snags developed, and if Borenboim had been a more perceptive man, he might have taken notice.

While Naum wandered around a department store during his lunch
hour, looking for a birthday present for Lily, by some miracle he avoided
coming face to face with his wife, Faina, who was being pushed and shoved
in a shampoo line. Then, at the end of the day, his boss invited the whole
staff out to dinner at the Metropole Restaurant to celebrate his birthday.
Borenboim stuttered something about his sick wife who expected him
home on time. "What are you worrying yourself about, Comrade Borenboim?" asked his boss. "I'll call up your respected spouse right now and get
her approval."

In a moment of panic, Naum blurted that the telephone had been disconnected for nonpayment and, to everyone's amazement, excused himself.

This is what happened next:

7:00 P.M.— Naum calls the apartment. Lily races to the telephone.
"She's gone," she whispers, and puts down the receiver.

7:30 P.M.— Naum enters the apartment through the back door and
secretly makes his way to the room of his beloved Lilichka.

11:00 P.M.— The light goes out in Lily's room, though music contin-
ues to play softly.

11:30 P.M.— Faina unexpectedly returns home after a wild argument
with her sister.

3:00 A.M.— Borenboim heads for the toilet.

3:05 A.M.— Borenboim leaves the toilet.

And here an evil spirit—also called the force of habit—played a dirty trick
on him. Instead of returning to Lily's room, the half-asleep lover mechani-
cally went into his own room.

A horrifying scream pierced the air of our Outstanding-Communist-
Way-of-Life-Apartment. Awakening from a light sleep, Faina shrieked frantically at the sight of a naked man. When she recognized the familiar torso,
her voice rose an octave.

We all turned on our lights and rushed into the corridor. Senka Roof
celebrated as though it were New Year's Eve and kicked on every door to
invite everybody to share in the festivities. Dressed in Naum's present, a
negligee from Poland, and looking like a young Greta Garbo, Lily froze,
covering her mouth with her hand. Poor Naum was hopping from one
foot to the other in the center of the storm, clutching his head and sputter-

ing, "Oh, God! It's not me . . . Faina, darling! Don't pay any attention to us . . . Don't believe your eyes, my dear!"

The next day, Faina submitted a report to the Leningrad Gas Company and also to the Housing Office, thereby supplying Naum and Lily's co-workers with many hours of amusement and joy. Borenboim got an official condemnation and was ordered to reconcile with his wife and make love to her. But Faina threw his suitcase out of the window and filed for divorce. Naum went to stay with a friend, Faina moved in with her sister, and their room was locked and silent. Lily, fearful of social branding, took a month off from work at her own expense and slipped away to the Crimea.

We had not yet recovered from this tumult when something happened that eclipsed Naum's tragic performance. Senka Roof and Vasili Bochkin . . . But here the Bochkin family should be properly introduced.

Vasili Bochkin, a heavy-jowled and ape-hairy man with a bit of gypsy blood in him, was usually drunk five days a week. Even a subtle hint to dry out sent him into a frenzy.

"I'm not a problem drinker," he would roar at his wife, Lyuba, the meekest of women, whom we nicknamed the Dove.

"Did you get that? Do you understand the difference between an alcoholic and a drunk? A drunk, that's what I am, get it? I drink for the joy of it, to release and express my eternal soul!"

Vasili Bochkin worked as a plumber at the Karl Marx candy factory. The sweet, pungent smell of chocolate followed him everywhere. Lyuba, a worker at the Friedrich Engels Tire Factory, always smelled of rubber. She was an inspector of fashionable galoshes. The couple lived on her wages; Vasili left his at the liquor store.

Whenever Bochkin felt that his immortal soul was still not sufficiently expressed, he would wheedle money out of his wife. Once in a while she would say no to him, and then Vasili would beat her till she was half dead. We would call the police, but the next morning Lyuba would powder her shiners and hurry to the police station, begging them to release her darling.

When she became pregnant, her dove's world view was changed, and she went to the candy factory to demand that Bochkin's salary be given directly to her. For Vasili, this loss of independence was a disaster. "Are you a man or a doormat?" his friend Senka Roof needled him. "She'll make an ass out of you."

Vasili would make a scene, manage to squeeze five rubles out of his wife, and disappear for forty-eight hours.

Once, just after the fall of the Borenboim family . . . But let us hear it in Vasili's own words. This is what he told a police investigator:

I felt lousy that day. I thought if I didn't get some booze real quick I'd die. My nerves strained to the limit. A human being feels like that sometimes. And I didn't have a kopeck in my pocket, and there was nowhere I could get any.

Vasili glanced at the investigator who nodded his head sympathetically.

So I dragged myself home, and my wife wasn't there yet. I dug around in the cupboard, under the mattress, went through all the dressers—nothing. I couldn't figure out where she was hiding it. And there was no one to borrow from. Naum and Faina had split up, and that bitch in heat, excuse the expression, Lily, had gone off to the South. My condition, Citizen Investigator, really stank, I couldn't see straight, my head was splitting, my throat felt dry, and I had nothing but blurry visions around me. And that sonofabitch Senka—excuse me, Comrade Senka Roof—hadn't got back from work yet, and all my hopes hung on him.

Then Lyuba came home, nasty as a witch. Since she got pregnant, you wouldn't even recognize her, not a hello or good-bye from her. She threw her purse on the bed and went into the kitchen. I made a mad dash for her handbag, turned it inside out, but nothing. Then she came back from the kitchen, and she said, to quote her exactly, "No bread. I'll go get some. Wait here. I'll be back, and then we'll eat."

I said to her, "Wait, Lyuba, I feel sick to my stomach."

"Stop guzzling," she said and slammed the door. I ran after her down the stairs.

"Lyuba," I said, "come on, give me a break and fork over three rubles!"

I remember precisely—I even put my arm around her. But she pulled away, her eyes all crazy, and snapped, "Go to hell," and she even, believe it or not, used dirty language at me.

"Lyuba," I said, "what's come over you? You never used to talk to me like that. For the last time, I'm begging you, please, otherwise, I'm not responsible what I'll do to myself . . ."

"So you threatened her?" the investigator interrupted.

No, I threatened me, not her! And she said, "Do what you want, go jump into the Neva River, or hang yourself."

I returned to our room like a beaten dog. Can you imagine that bitch, going on like that? "Hang yourself," she said. And if I did, I'd like to see how she would bring up our child without a father.

The picture of a fatherless child upset Vasili so much that he sobbed, and the investigator hurried to him with a glass of water.

To tell the truth, I wasn't intending to hang myself entirely—just enough to make my point. I'm not a monster, after all, to leave a kid without a daddy. I just decided to give Lyuba a little scare. I took a rope, wound it around my neck and then under my arms, and put my jacket over it so she wouldn't see it. There was no decent hook in our room, but there were three good ones in the bathroom for the clothesline. I picked the strongest-looking one, slipped the noose around my neck, climbed onto the edge of the tub, and waited for her to come in. The only thing I was afraid of was falling into the tub, because there was all this underwear soaking in it. Suddenly I heard her steps. I jumped off and hung there. The rope scraped my neck a little, but I managed hanging there perfectly alright. I pretended to be dead, rolled back my eyes, and stuck out my tongue. Now, I thought, she'll poke her nose in here, and I'll get a look at her . . .

I heard footsteps coming down the hall. Just as I planned, she stopped at the bathroom door. Then I saw out of the corner of my eye that it was not Lyuba, but my very best friend, Senka Roof. He stared at me, his eyes bulging out of his head. Hell, I thought, the whole thing is ruined. He's bound to yell like a madman and spoil the whole effect. I even closed my eyes tight, but that's not what happened.

Comrade Roof locked the door and jumped on me. Imagine, Citizen Investigator, Comrade Roof turned my pockets inside out. He groped around in my jacket and pants pockets. It tickled very much. Then he grabbed my hand and took off my watch. It was a present from my mother, and I [here Vasili's voice trembled] I never, no matter how much I needed money, ever even thought of selling it. So I got so mad, so furious, so outraged—this man, you understand, was supposed to be my best buddy, robbing a hanging man blind—that I kicked Roof in the stomach with my foot. And then that damn fool had the gall to croak on me right there.

This happened at 6 P.M. We suddenly heard an agonizing cry and the sound of a falling body coming from behind the bathroom door. We tried to open it, but it was locked. We broke in. Vasili Bochkin was swinging on a hook, trying to reach the edge of the bathtub with his feet, while Senka Roof lay on the floor, wheezing, with Bochkin's watch clutched in his hand. The ambulance arrived with lightning speed, but it was too late. Comrade Roof never regained consciousness and died of a heart attack on the way to the hospital.

Then silence and tranquillity finally settled over our apartment. Naum and Faina Borenboim were nowhere to be seen; Lily Kuzina was sitting out the scandal in the Crimea; Comrade Roof was pushing up the daisies; Vasili Bochkin was locked up with the criminally insane; and dove-like Lyuba had gone to her mother's to deliver her fatherless baby.

And due to the idyllic calm, we finally won the honorable title of the Outstanding-Communist-Way-of-Life-Apartment.

8 A Woman, Fortyish, with Acne

When I was a high school student, I used to get the highest grades in psychology, social studies, and history, and the lowest in physics and chemistry. I loved literature and languages but hated math. I didn't care about making scientific discoveries or searching for minerals. Even less did I want to spend the best years of my life in field expeditions, living in tents among bears, ticks, and mosquitoes. And yet I chose geology as my profession and wound up at the Mining Institute, the most "masculine" of all colleges. How come?

I think that my major motivation was to do everything I could to spite my nature, to prove to myself and to the rest of mankind that the word *impossible* is not in my vocabulary. "There are no limits to what we can do at sea and on land"—so goes the famous Communist "March of the Enthusiasts," and I made those words my motto.

Every summer and fall the students of the geology department worked in field expeditions, far away from home. After the freshman year, when I was only eighteen, I was sent to work in Karelia for four months. "I'll have a life full of adventures, challenges, and dangers. It's s-o-o-o romantic," I bragged to my friends. "Don't you envy me?" I assume they did.

For the fifth day in a row I found myself wandering in a Karelian forest of fallen trees in a perpetual drizzle. Our padded cotton jackets were soaking wet. For four nights we had slept on the ground in the forest, and we had eaten our last hot meal two days before. And *that,* truth be told, was all my fault. While fording the rapids of a mountain stream, Osinka, I had slipped on a log and did a belly flop into the icy water. I was fished out with the help of a few long branches, but my backpack full of canned goods and bread drowned somewhere downstream.

"Never mind, Countess," Valya Gromov, the chief geologist, consoled me. "Just be glad that you're in one piece." He walked ahead of us, carrying the almost unliftable knapsack that held our geological samples. Disheveled curls and phenomenal endurance gave Valya an uncanny resemblance to a wild horse. Next came our geophysicist, Leo Ryabushkin, a chubby-cheeked burly guy with a thick mustache. Leo was slung with daters and bores, and a Geiger counter dangled from his pocket. I trailed at the rear.

It seemed that the forest was populated by nothing but mosquitoes and gnats. Our faces were swathed in green netting that reeked of insect repellent. We wore helmets, gloves up to our elbows, and rubber hip boots. This was all by way of antimosquito defense, but we were still being attacked in droves. I was woozy from hunger, and my ears were ringing. If I ever tripped, I would never get up again.

"Cheer up, monkey!" Valya turned around. "In an hour we'll reach the dirt road."

And so our journey was coming to an end. Behind us lay a hundred and twenty miles of surveying. Hundreds of samples, including dozens of pounds of sand rinsed in icy streams, weighed heavily on Valya's bent back. The expedition's pick-up truck was supposed to meet us at the road and drive us another forty miles to the base camp.

"What do you think? Has Peter come?" I asked woefully. Leo shrugged his shoulders. Valya didn't answer at all. We all knew very well that ever since the head of the expedition, an aging Madame, had made Peter her beaux, he had gone to pot.

"Come, come, Peter, darling, never you mind." We could imagine the tender whisper of our boss coming from the general's tent. "Have a drink and relax. Don't you worry about them. These field geologists are as strong as mules. Their legs won't fall off if they walk back all the way."

So there we were, finally at the road—and no trace of Peter of course. We collapsed at the side of the road and tuned out. An hour later, Valya shook us back to life.

"Let's go. Let's head for the station and see if we can hitch a ride home."

"Swear to God, I'm going to break that bastard Peter's legs," said Leo phlegmatically. "If he doesn't give a damn about us, he could at least have taken pity on the girl."

It was about five miles to the railroad station, but we were so wiped out we barely made it. When we finally saw the lights of Losevka it was already growing dark. On the tracks, all set to depart, was a very long freight train loaded with timber.

"Will you look at that? Maybe there is a God after all!" cried Leo.

"Don't rush," said Valya. "Let's circle around to make sure that some jerk doesn't try to cut us off at the platform."

We skirted the rear end of the train and scrambled onto a landing between two cars. Almost immediately, as if the train had been waiting for us, a whistle came from the direction of the platform, and the cars with a clank and a squeal began to move.

"Some dumb luck, huh?" Leo grinned, making himself comfortable. "Riding like kings!"

After about an hour and a half the freight train slowed down.

"Folks, we're coming into Sheltozero," shouted Valya. "The platform will be on the right. Prepare to descend on the left."

The train gave a jerk and came to a dead halt. Our car seemed to be the last one; the lights from the platform shone far ahead. It was pitch dark all around us. Suddenly we heard people running toward us, and we were blinded by high beams.

"Hands up!" We were surrounded on both sides of the car by soldiers carrying machine guns.

Clumsily, like sacks of potatoes, we jumped down to the ground. Someone poked his rifle butt into my back, and our hands went up. "Take off your guns, and put them down by your feet!" an officer snarled.

Leo stood still, his geophysical instruments hanging all over him, and blinked in dismay.

"Lieutenant Kurochkin, translate."

A skinny type in glasses stepped forward, and in a slow, distinct voice pronounced something in an absolutely unfamiliar language. Valya spluttered a laugh; Leo still hadn't moved a muscle. "Leo, take off that harness," Valya said. Leo started to unhitch his straps slowly.

"Do you understand Russian?" The captain turned sharply to Valya.

"Quite, although we don't understand what you want from us."

Leo carefully placed the instruments on the ground. Three soldiers bent over and started examining the dater and bore. "What's that?"

"An RP-l, a geophysical instrument used for detecting uranium," Leo offered. "It doesn't shoot."

"That's for us to decide!" the officer bellowed. "Follow me."

They led us along the entire length of the train. Ahead, close to the locomotive, stood two army jeeps. We were prodded into a jeep, and four guards jauntily hopped up onto the running board. Two minutes later the jeep stopped in front of a long barrack, about three hundred yards from the station.

"Where are you taking us?" Leo asked.

"The Railroad Division of the regional KUKGB," the officer growled.

"KU—what?" Leo had not heard him. "KU—you know what!" Valya whispered from behind.

We were taken into a room with green walls, two safes, and a desk from above which, exactly like family portraits, Lenin and Dzerzhinsky (the fathers of the Soviet Union and of the KGB, respectively) gazed down at us severely. Opposite, as if anticipating his own short public life, hung a lonely portrait of Nikita Khrushchev.

We were ordered to stand against the wall. The three soldiers stationed themselves by the entrance. The officer threw off his overcoat and cap and sat down at his desk.

"Captain Dyomin," he finally introduced himself, and, taking out some blanks from the desk drawer, he turned to Valya.

"Last name, first name, date of birth."

"I'm not going to answer your questions," Valya said quietly, "until you explain what you're arresting us for."

"We're not arresting you, we're temporarily detaining you. For the time being, for traveling on freight train #A18–462 from Losevka station. You boarded at 18:20 and were detained at the Sheltozero Station at 20:03."

"The hell we were detained. We arrived, that's all. Our base camp is nearby. We're geologists from Leningrad."

"And where's this camp of yours?" The captain squinted at us.

"Past Gavrilino, about eight miles from here."

"Gavrilino is fifteen miles from here by road and eleven miles through the woods. So you've got your facts slightly screwed up."

"Maybe, but there's no reason for hauling us into the KGB."

"There's plenty of reason," Dyomin snapped. "And if you really are geologists, then what were you doing hiding and sneaking around? Why didn't you travel like normal people, by passenger train?"

"What passenger train?" Valya asked.

"Passenger train #311 and the express train #46 pass through Losevka at 8:05 and 11:16 in the morning." The captain spoke in the clipped tones of an information bureau. He cast an eagle eye over us.

"But it's nighttime now!" exclaimed Valya. "Nighttime, understand? Put us in touch with our base this instant!"

"Hold on, cut that yowling!" the captain roared and bared his yellow fangs. "We'll get in touch with them if and when I say so. Now, your last name, first name, and your passport."

Valya did not answer. His lips were trembling.

"What would we be doing with our passports in the forest?" Leo asked calmly. "You know as well as I that our papers are kept at the base for security reasons."

"What's the phone number at your base?" The fangs were covered.

"There's no phone there," I chimed in. "Our base is in the middle of the woods, we live in tents; but it is really quite close. Let's all go there together right now."

"We'll go there if and when I say so," Dyomin cut me off. "And now I'm asking you again, for the last time: your last name, first name, and date of birth."

Once he had learned our biographies five generations back, Dyomin ordered us to sign our testimonies.

"Well, now can we go?" Valya made a move toward the door. The captain nailed him to the spot with a glance.

"Until your identities have been confirmed, you will stay here. Abdulaev, take the suspects away."

The bow-legged Uzbek led us to the end of the corridor and opened the padlock on one of the doors. We found ourselves in a cell with four plank beds and a tiny light bulb suspended from the ceiling. We were dying to use the toilet, dying for something to eat and drink.

"What about some grub?" Leo inquired curtly.

Abdulaev did not respond. He went out, closed the door, and snapped the lock shut.

"What are you, deaf or something?" Valya exploded. "Goddamned cross-eyed bastard!" And he kicked the door with all his might.

"Cool it," Leo hushed him. "Or they will tack on 'racism.'"

But Valya had gone utterly berserk. He pounded on the door and hollered: "Let us out to use the toilet! Hear me?"

The lock clattered, and our "brother" appeared on the threshold. "I'll take you one at a time," he said and pointed a finger at me. "You first." When we had finished with the toilet, the Uzbek locked the door again and vanished. We lay down on our cots and, strangely enough, quickly dropped off to sleep.

At six in the morning a red-haired soldier appeared at our door. "Rise and shine!" he shouted cheerfully and brought in mugs of boiling water and three pieces of bread.

"Hi there, pal! What's your name?"

"Private Bulkin, Pavel Bulkin."

"Listen, friend Pavel, what's the word out there? Did they send somebody to our base?"

"Who the hell knows?" Bulkin shrugged his shoulders.

"Did they call Leningrad, our headquarters?"

"I believe they did, but no one answered. The captain says you're all lying, there is no such phone number."

"Lord," moaned Leo. "It was nighttime, and today's Saturday. Nobody's there. But why for God's sake didn't they get in touch with our base camp?"

"Who the fuck knows," Pavel said gleefully. "Come on, don't get so worked up. Dig in."

In the afternoon he brought us a few bluish-black boiled potatoes and plunked himself down next to us on a bunk.

"Pavlusha," Valya began intimately. "I can see you're a decent guy, not like some people . . ." He thrust out his lower jaw and drew his eyes into a slant with his fingers. Bulkin guffawed appreciatively. "You must be up on things, friend. Why has Dyomin latched on to us? Surely not because we hitched a ride?"

Private Bulkin shook his head. On his dopey face a fierce struggle was being played out between his military duty, his compassion, and his simple urge to shoot the breeze.

"You see, this is the thing . . ." Finally, Pavel could not stand it any more. "We're on the lookout for spies."

Valya let out a long whistle. "Spies?! What does that have to do with us?"

"Well, there are three spies in the area—two men and a woman. And all the particulars match up—one guy with a mustache, and a woman, fortyish, with acne."

"Wha-a-t? Do I look forty? And acne?"

Bulkin looked embarrassed. "What are you getting so worked up about? How should I know? I didn't look at your passport."

Valya collapsed on his bunk in laughter. "Pavel, let us out of here right now so you don't make fools of yourselves."

"Are you out of your mind or something?" Bulkin blew up. "Sit down and shut up."

"I'll shut up, all right," Valya reassured him, "but where did these spies supposedly come from?"

"Finland, where else? The day before yesterday our forester came tearing in here all lathered up. 'Spies,' he says, 'I saw three spies with my very own eyes. They crossed the border from Finland somewhere around Post #7.' And then there you were, crawling out of the woods right at Losevka and sneaking onto the freight train."

"You mean someone saw us in Losevka?"

"Sure! Everyone saw you, but they were afraid of startling you."

"And they even noticed that the woman had acne?"

"Yup! And they phoned to all the stations along the way and decided to take you off the train in Sheltozero. They skipped two stations—Sergeevka and Uglino—because the forest's so close there you could get away."

"Super-fucking-amazing!" Valya was beside himself. "Well, you are wonder workers! What do you think? Are you going to get a medal for capturing us or an extra vacation?"

"Yeah, sure," Pavel was pleased that he got it all out, but suddenly checked himself. "Medal or no medal, we're just doing our job. So go on, relax." He collected the mugs and hurried to get out, embarrassed by his own candor.

"Hey, guys!" Leo looked very alarmed. "That is some kind of gobbledygook! Let's demand to see Dyomin."

But no one responded to our shouts and banging. In the evening Private Abdulaev came to watch us again. All attempts to make friendly contact with him ended in disaster. And the next morning Bulkin came back.

"Pavel, dear," Valya said tenderly, "what's the news?"

"What more news do you want?" Bulkin grumbled. He was out of sorts.

"Call Dyomin, please, we need to talk."

"Where am I going to get him for you on a Sunday? We're not expecting the captain here until tomorrow."

"What do you mean? We've got to stay here today, too?" Leo leapt up.

"People stay locked up for twenty years in a row, no big deal," the youthful Bulkin informed us, shutting the door behind himself.

"Good Lord!" Leo cracked each of his ten fingers consecutively. "We could vegetate here for twenty years."

"Don't panic, old buddy," Valya said. "It's not Stalin's era anymore. The times have changed, thank God."

"Maybe we should go on a hunger strike?" I suggested.

"What a brilliant idea!" Valya laughed. "When Dyomin learns that we've refused the filet minion he'll get terribly depressed."

"But we have to do something!"

"Well . . . I'm thinking about sending Private Bulkin to the store. I could use something to eat, and a drink wouldn't be bad either." Valya waved a red ten-ruble bill in front of our noses. "Pretty sloppy workers here. They didn't take away my capital."

When Bulkin reappeared with his multicolored potatoes, Valya was meek as a lamb. "Pavel, my dear friend, run over to the store and buy us some tobacco and a few cans of food."

Bulkin pointed to his temple and twisted his finger expressively. "Hey pal, what the hell . . . Are you nuts?"

"Look, you know we're not spies. There's no reason for holding us."

"If there isn't, then they'll let you go, right?"

"Yeah, and in the meantime we're twiddling our thumbs. Listen, what if you let me go alone while you keep them under strict guard?"

"And where are you thinking of going?"

"I told you—to the store. To buy cigarettes and something halfway decent to eat."

"There hasn't been anything halfway decent to eat in that store in a hundred years," Bulkin assured us, "so there's no point in wearing out your shoes." However, the expression on his face gave us a glimmer of hope.

"Pavel, brother, you're a Russian soul, you're one in a million," Valya persisted. "Let me out for fifteen minutes—five to the store, five back, and five there."

Bulkin heaved a sigh. He was a picture of goodness, sympathy, and compassion shadowed by indecision.

"What's there to worry about? You said so yourself, Dyomin's not going to be here today," Valya insisted.

"Get going," Bulkin suddenly made up his mind, "but you sure as hell better be back in fifteen minutes."

Valya came back right on the dot, carrying a loaf of bread, two cans of fish in tomato sauce, and a pack of cigarettes. Something long, wrapped up in newspaper, stuck out from under his elbow.

"What's that?" I pointed to the parcel.

"That? Kielbasa . . . Ukrainian smoked kielbasa."

"Kielbasa?!" Bulkin gasped. "Kielbasa in that store?" He leaped up as if he'd been stung and vanished, not even stopping to close the door behind him. We stared at each other.

"Lady and gentlemen," Valya's head cleared, "it looks like we are no longer being detained." He poked his head out into the corridor and beckoned to us with his finger.

"Well, then, let's split."

We scrambled out of the cell, and Leo cautiously clicked the lock. The corridor was empty. We slithered out on tiptoe, being careful not to make the floor creak, and came out onto the street. Not a soul in sight. Then and there we broke into a run. Looping in and out between the storage sheds, we jumped over the railroad tracks and dashed through a sparse patch of woods before rolling head over heels into a sandpit. A forty-ton truck loaded with sand was just crawling out of there. We waved to the driver. The driver stuck his head out. "Where're you headed, guys?"

"To Gavrilino, or in that direction at least."

"The Kilsk Cement Factory okay?"

We nodded and crowded into the cab. The truck slowly picked up speed.

"Where are you coming from all decked out like that?" the driver inquired, taking in our rags and my friends' overgrown pusses.

"From the woods. We're geologists."

"And the girl, what's she, a geologess? Whadaya know," chuckled the driver.

I stuck my head out of the cab—nope, no one in pursuit.

Remembering Valya's package and breaking off a hunk of bread in anticipation, Leo suggested, "Hey, let's have that kielbasa of yours."

"The Ukrainian smoked kielbasa, you mean?" Valya solemnly removed the newspaper wrapping. A bottle of pepper vodka gleamed right under our noses.

"Well, aren't you smarter than hell?" Leo was impressed.

The driver gazed lovingly at the vodka. Valya pulled the aluminum cap off with his teeth and passed the bottle around. After four full rounds, it flew out the window, crashed against a boulder, and shattered into a million pieces.

"Has anyone given any thought to Private Bulkin's tragic fate?" Leo asked, "I don't know about you, but my heart is bleeding."

"They won't do a damn thing to him. In the worst case, he'll sit in the guardhouse for a couple of weeks for being so scatter-brained," I said. "Especially taking into consideration the fact that I am not yet forty years old and do not have acne, his punishment shouldn't be very severe."

"People stay locked up for twenty years in a row, no big deal," Valya quoted maliciously.

We had a smoke, then closed our eyes and dozed off. An hour later, the truck stopped in front of the gates of the Kilsk Cement Factory.

"Thanks so very, very much!" We were ready to jump off, but the driver did not let us out.

"How far is your base?"

"Four miles, not a big deal," Valya said.

"Wait." The driver pulled back, and, in a gesture of brotherly love, he drove that hulk of his to Gavrilino and stepped on the brakes near our tents.

"Thanks, pal. You are our hero." Valya dug in his pocket and took out a ruble.

"Don't the fuck offend me. I didn't do it for money," the driver said, pushing away Valya's hand. "I did it because I wanted to."

It was a peaceful Sunday at base camp. An evening mist crept over the lake. A boat carrying two motionless figures rocked near the shore: our lady-boss and Peter were fishing. From the farthest tent came the static of a shortwave radio, and then a distinct, but slightly accented, Russian: "With this we close our weekly survey, 'The View from London.'" Several people were playing cards by the camp fire. When one of them, Boris, the cook, saw us, he let out a Tarzan yell. Our colleagues jumped up, giving us their places by the fire. Peter rowed to shore, and the authorities greeted us with a sweet smile.

"So, our lost sheep have returned," Madame said in a motherly voice. "And I was just thinking where could they have vanished?"

I dove into my tent. My sleeping bag was turned inside out, my suitcase upturned, and someone else's comb was on the nightstand.

"Hey!" I shouted, "Who's been messing around with my stuff?"

"Oh, I completely forgot," the boss said. "We had guests, mushroom hunters. They got lost in the forest. They wandered around for two days and came to our camp at night. What were we supposed to do with them? We let them spend the night. They were from Petrozavodsk, workers from a lumber yard. Two men and a woman. So we let the woman have your tent . . . No objections, I hope?"

"Of course, not, it was very kind of you."

"My dear comrades!" Our lady said, suddenly alarmed, "Why have you come back empty-handed? Where are your samples? Where are your instruments?"

"Everything's all right," Valya reported. "We left it all for safekeeping at the Sheltozero Railroad KGB Division with a friend of mine, Major Dyomin. Would you, please, drive over and pick it up?"

"Oh, shit! What a nuisance!" The boss clapped her hands. "We just came from there an hour ago."

"You weren't going to meet us?" Leo asked genteelly.

"Why should we meet you? You're not children, you know your way. No, we were driving the mushroom hunters back. We barely made it in time for the express to Petrozavodsk."

"Yeah, a bunch of dummies," Peter piped in. "They didn't know the forest and had no sense of direction at all. They should've stayed home and picked their mushrooms at the market."

"What did they look like, these mushroom hunters of yours?" Valya pricked up his ears.

"Nothing special. The guys were young, and the woman was a little older, I'd say."

"That woman, by the way, was a real fright," Boris the cook interrupted, as he ladeled steaming Ukranian borscht into our mugs: "You know, fortyish, with acne."

9 The Day of the Iron

The wide corridor outside of the dean's offices on the third floor of the Mining Institute was the main artery for all our comings and goings. It has long been known as a place for "accidental" meetings and planned rendezvous. In breaks between classes, we loved to wander back and forth past the dean's offices or sit on the windowsills, both to show ourselves off and to check out everyone else. Vitally important encounters, partings, and discussions of personal relationships took place in this "Dean's Corridor."

Once, my attention was drawn to a thin, shaggy, and bespectacled student. He was dressed in the institute's uniform with gold shoulder straps, a chicken-like neck stuck out from a collar that was too wide, and on his shoulders hung a backpack. "The epitome of a perfect student," I thought to myself. Later I spotted him in the institute's museum, in the library, and then in the cafeteria—this time not alone but with my friend Jack Sukhanov. I apologized, took Jack to the side, and whispered into his ear: "Would you introduce me to this guy in glasses? But, please, be discreet, just act casually."

"Of course, no problem . . . Tolya!" he shouted out. "Someone's dying to meet you over here!"

Everyone in line turned as if on command. The young man came up. He had a birthmark on his upper lip, very white, straight teeth, and his entire being lit up in a smile . . . or something lit up in me.

"Tanya Verhovskaya, the institute's champion in the hundred-meter crawl, wants to meet you," said Jack, marvelously demonstrating the art of diplomacy. "And this is my friend Tolya Dargis, straight-A student and the pride of our group."

"You mean, the disgrace of your group," I cleverly parried.

They didn't catch the irony in my attack, and no one countered. An awkward silence set in. Tolya Dargis looked at me patiently and smiled.

"What, in particular, strikes you as being so funny?" I said, just asking for trouble.

"Tanya, have you ever been *in a jam?*"

I instead heard *with a man.*

"With a man? Have I ever been with a man?" I let out a fatal laugh. "Hundreds of times. That's all I ever do . . ."

And again a silence set in, one that I simply could not endure.

"Why don't we go to the Frog to celebrate getting our stipends?"

In our student years, the Nord and the Frog were the only decent cafes in Leningrad. The Nord was priced out of our range, but the Frog was very reasonable. The seats there were covered in green velvet, and sparkling wine, ice cream, and iced coffee were served.

"Why not? Let's go," said Jack.

"Unfortunately I can't," Tolya said, looking at his watch. "I'm busy. I am meeting someone at the tram stop in fifteen minutes."

"What, you can't change your meeting?"

"I can't, and, more importantly, I do not want to."

Such audacity was unheard of. Well, who does he think he is? He, you see, is busy. And just look, he has a meeting! He ought to be in seventh heaven that I honored him with my attention. (The idea that I was the smartest, most beautiful, and most talented creature around has been ingrained in me since childhood like an indisputable scientific fact.) A hunter's instinct had awakened in me. Watching his back as he walked away, I swore that in less than a week Anatoly Dargis will surrender to my charms.

I spent the entire evening thinking up various plots for the grand seduction, but my mind's eye saw his soft smile, my ears heard his soft voice, and all my plans turned to dust. On the following day I looked up his schedule on the bulletin board and memorized it, and after classes I caught his eye.

"Hi, Tolya. You haven't, by any chance, seen Jack? I desperately need to speak with him."

"He was just here. Shall I call him?" And off he went in search of Jack, whom I needed like hole in the head.

In five minutes they showed up together, and I invited them to the Hermitage for the Picasso exhibit, the most talked-about event in Leningrad's cultural life in the past sixty years. Tolya said that he had seen this exhibit the day before and that it would be a shame if I missed it . . . Burning with spite, I trudged along with Jack to the Hermitage to feast my eyes on that wretched Picasso for the third time.

The next day I invited Tolya again, this time to the party held by my Department of Geology. Each year competitive departments had parties at which plays were performed, skits were put on, and orchestras were invited to play. The administration of the Mining Institute, reputed for its continued liberal traditions, allowed the students to parody their professors and, for the more courageous, to recognize certain faults of the system. To attend the party of another department was practically impossible, for tickets were distributed to local trade union committees, among the elite, or acquired through high connections. My department's parties were known for being the most maverick and the most intellectual because of the fine poets and writers who emerged from its depths. I got hold of two tickets and again set up a trap for Tolya in the Dean's Corridor.

"Would you like to go to our party on Saturday?"

"Do you really have extra tickets?"

"There are no *extra* tickets. I have my own."

"Does that mean that I would have to go with you?"

Unheard-of insolence . . . It would have cost anyone else their head.

"You don't have to do anything. You may take anyone you like with you."

"Thank you very much. That is so kind of you. We've been dying to get into your geological party."

Who is *we,* who, for God's sake, is this *we?* I hoped that *we* meant himself and Jack.

Tolya Dargis arrived at the party with a gaunt brunette. She was shapeless like the ladies of Picasso's paintbrush. She wore a white sweater and a red-checked skirt, had pretty legs, a wasp's waist, and a disproportionately long neck, for which I was quick to dub her "Nessy." This nickname stubbornly stuck with her for years and carried across oceans and continents.

When the dances began and the ladies' tango was announced, I sprung on Tolya like a panther and tore him out of Nessy's arms.

"Well, Tolya, how did you like our concert? Not too boring, I hope?"

"Are you kidding? Not at all."

"Then why do you have this boring look about you, that is, a look as if you are bored?"

"On the contrary, I'm very happy."

"But you have such a bored look on your face today," I persisted.

"I'm afraid that is not something I can help," Tolya said dryly, and he did not utter a word for the rest of the tango.

Ten minutes later he and his Nessy left, at which time I huddled in the cloakroom and sobbed through the rest of the night.

A week passed, then two, three. Tolya Dargis still had not given in to my charms. I discovered that he loved music and subscribed to the Bach concert series. That year I got my fill of masses and fugues by frequenting the conservatory. The moment I entered the vestibule I could feel his presence. The chandeliers shone brighter, the crowd looked more festive, the ushers were friendlier, and the air was charged with a million protons and electrons. Every cell of my skin sensed his presence. Sometimes he came with Nessy. At these times we nodded ceremoniously to one another during the intermission. Other times, when he was alone, we came out onto the hazy Theater Square after the concert. No, he did not escort me; we simply were headed in the same direction. A month later I stopped eating, sleeping, and studying. I sat through the lectures in a haze, carefully tracing on the edges of my notebooks "T.D.," "Anatoly D.," "A. Dargis," "Anatol" . . .

I became so desperate that I joined a scientific society chaired by Tolya and did a presentation on one of the most obscure nineteenth-century round-the-world expeditions, that of two Russian scientists, Kruzenshtern and Lisyansky.

Is there a limit to the madness love is capable of producing? Tolya congratulated me on a job well done, but this was no cause for celebration. It turned out that Scottish Nessy was a poetess and a member of the literary union. I almost composed "The Song of Hiawatha" just to spite her. I made a sad attempt to crush my rival by letting out word that she had a wooden leg. It was obvious foolishness, for she was our top gymnast. I suffered defeat after defeat, until one day . . .

Somehow Tolya let it slip that he really wanted to read a book by Dos Passos but could not get it because no library in Leningrad had it.

"No problem," I said carelessly. "I have one sitting on my shelf."

"Really? Could you bring it to the institute tomorrow, just for a few days?"

"Why not come over to my place?"

"I'd be happy to. At what time?"

"Now, immediately, right this very second!" I wanted to shout, but instead said, "Tomorrow, around three, if you can."

There were no Dos Passos books in the house. I called everybody—acquaintances, friends, and enemies. The novel *The 42nd Parallel* was in the hands of Papa's friend Professor Samarin.

"I will not permit you to take it out of the house," he said. "Come on over and read it all you like. But not a step further, for I'm already missing half of my home library."

I hassled the professor until he allowed me to take the book for three days and then rushed to Pavlovsk to get it. I drank juice with his partially deaf mother-in-law; listened to tales about their cat, Alice, and spaniel, Turandot; retold the plot of Greta Garbo's *Queen Christina;* swore that I would guard the book with my life; and, at last, pressing Dos Passos to my bosom, barely caught the last train. When I returned home I discovered that *The 42nd Parallel* was not in my bag. Where could I have left it? I called the taxi garage, went to the bureau of lost and found at Vitebsk Station, argued with my parents, and cried until dawn. In the morning I called around until I was able to get the book seller Arkasha Busin on the phone and begged him to dig out *The 42nd Parallel* from under the earth before three o'clock at any cost.

"What do you mean, at any cost?" Busin said. "I'm not a gangster. A used Dos Passos costs three hundred bucks. Come on over." Three hundred bucks was about my monthly scholarship.

I did not go to class. Instead I dashed to the ends of the earth to our Nulya, my former nanny, the only person in the world who would lend me money, no questions asked. Then to Busin, to the hairdresser, to the Nord for pastry, to Yeliseyevsky for roast beef and smoked salmon, and to the market for flowers—all by taxi.

By two o'clock the apartment was spotless, the floors had been scrubbed, and the scent of lilies permeated the air.

"The Inspector General is coming," Papa said phlegmatically.

I snapped back and pretended that I was reading a paleontology textbook. At two thirty Papa glanced into my room.

"I hope you appreciate our tact. I am leaving for a department meeting, and your mother is going to the publishing house. But we could stay home . . . if you like . . . It's too bad we have no harp; you could really use a harp now. Or a lute."

"Don't tease the tiger," my mother said from the hallway.

Three o'clock came and went, then four, half past four . . . At first I tried to read the blasted *Parallel,* but the letters scattered away like ants. Then I sat on the chair in the hallway so that I could hear the entrance door open and close. There, footsteps reverberated . . . *His* footsteps . . . *He* is ringing the bell . . .

On the landing stood Mama's friend Sophia Borisovna, known in our family as Baba Yaga . . . She looked like a blond Halloween witch with heavy make-up and a hooked nose. Papa could do a marvelous imitation of her shrill voice and her habit of asking the most idiotic questions at a rate of approximately forty per minute. Mama fervently defended her: "Sophia is a good and decent person."

And so, on the landing stood this good and decent person. Why did she always have to come at the worst times and without any warning?

"Hello, Tatochka. Is your mama home?"

"Unfortunately, no," I said, guarding the door behind me, like a goal-keeper.

"But where did she go off to?"

"I have not a slightest idea . . ." She took a step forward while I, of course, took one back.

"What? She left and did not say where she was going?" With just a gentle shove Sophia wound up in the foyer.

"Didn't say a word."

"How strange. I would never do such a thing. Gulya and Nolik always know where to find me," she said as she unbuttoned her coat.

"Sophia Borisovna, I am very busy."

"When did she leave?"

"Two hours ago."

"And when is she coming back?"

I demonstrated unusual restraint by merely shrugging my shoulders.

"You know, honey, I think I will wait for her. To get out of our remote neck of the woods is such a hassle, and I happened to be just around the corner from you. You don't mind, do you?"

Every conceivable method of torture and execution whirled around in my brain: quartering, impaling on a stake, hanging by the legs . . . I was sizzling with pure hatred.

"And sweetie, could you put the kettle on? I have not had a drop of anything since this morning."

Wishing she would drop dead, preferably in pangs and convulsions, I trudged off to the kitchen. Baba Yaga followed behind.

"So honey, how are you doing at the institute? My Nolik is struggling with his term project."

"Excuse me, Sophia Borisovna, but I must do some ironing."

"Sweet pea, we're just like family. Don't you pay me any mind . . ."

I went to the bathroom to iron. We had no ironing board, so I laid a drawing board on the edge of the tub and put a flannel blanket over it. The board covered half of the tub, so that it was still possible to climb into the other half. I turned on the iron and began to press a blouse. Sophia stood at the door and droned on about a "darling little blue dress" that she found in a department store for her daughter, that idiot Guli . . . I was afraid that I was going to split her head with the iron.

"Sophia Borisovna, could you sit in the other room? I want to take a shower."

"Do you really feel that self-conscious around me, hun? But then again, all children are the same, Guli throws me out of the room as well . . . Alright, I'm going . . .

I latched the door with the hook, undressed, ran the hot water, and slid into the remaining half of the tub. At last I had found a place where I could indulge myself in grief with no onlookers. Why didn't he come? Tears mixed with the hot stream of water flowed nonstop, and I did not hear the doorbell ring.

"Don't worry, I'll get it," Baba Yaga sang out from behind the door, and suddenly I heard Tolya's voice.

"Excuse me, please, is Tanya home?"

I jumped up so suddenly that I upset the drawing board, and the scorching iron flew down on my wet back. I gasped from pain and the sound of my own scream. I cannot remember in what order everything happened. Sophia Borisovna chirped piercingly. Tolya broke the bathroom door down and tore the iron from my back together with tatters of skin and flesh. Then came the ambulance, then my parents . . . Even now, twenty-five years later, a "special mark" remains on my back, a brown stain the size and shape of an electric iron.

The Day of the Iron went down in history as the beginning of our romance. For the first three weeks it proceeded at the hospital's trauma center. Tolya visited me every day, dragging with him, as Papa put it, "a whole greenhouse." On the day of my discharge from the hospital he came along with my parents to get me. After we had lunch, he proposed. I accepted. Keeping to custom, I asked only that Tolya speak with my parents. Father had gone to his study to take a nap; Mother sat by the telephone, calling friends to inform them of the happy ending of the iron episode. Tolya circled around her to seize a moment between calls, while from pure fear I ran outside. Right when Mother put the phone down on the hook Tolya took a deep breath and blurted out, "Natalya Pavlovna, I would like to ask your daughter for your hand . . ."

Mother choked and, howling from laughter, banged her head on the phone.

"Tolya, I am, well . . . sort of married . . ."

Actually, both my parents greeted the news as if it were a national disaster. Nulya, who was called upon to help them, stuck up for me: "I cannot fathom what you two are in such a tizzy about. You moan and groan, but it's time for the girl to get married. The boy, you say, is pretty ugly—looks like a real nerd. But then again, he's Jewish, so he's probably got a good brain in that head. And it looks like he doesn't drink. Some women end up marrying serial killers . . . So no big deal. They'll live, raise children . . ."

We handed our documents to the registry office in the middle of May, and we were to sign them on the first of June. Looking at my parents' sorrowful faces, we decided not to push for a formal wedding and postponed our honeymoon until the fall.

On the eve of our marriage registration, my parents said that they would not go to the registry with us because they could not bear seeing their "only daughter all of a sudden . . ."

"But I love him!" I shouted.

"So what? So you love him. Big deal," they answered in chorus. "Does that mean you have to rush off and marry him?"

When it was close to one in the afternoon and we were getting ready to go and register, their consciences took over. With blank faces but in formal attire they paced the apartment looking at their watches. Tolya Dargis did not show up at one, two, or three o'clock. Their faces lit up. Papa's brother Victor Ivanovich called every fifteen minutes to ask if the groom had "slit his wrists" already. Even now, as we approach our silver wedding anniversary, I grow cold with the memory of that day. But we must give credit to the strength of Tolya's character. In twenty-five years, in spite of entreaties, threats, and fist fights, he still has not learned *ever* to arrive *anywhere* on time.

The registry closed at five o'clock. Tolya Dargis showed up at seven with a basket of heavenly white roses.

"Excuse me. It seems I am a bit late," he said meekly. "I had a long way to go . . . I brought these roses from Kolpino."

My romantic Mama sobbed, "You brought these roses from heaven . . . ," and kissed Tolya on the nose.

Gradually, uninvited guests started to drop by. First Victor Ivanovich arrived with a bottle of champagne, a slide rule, and a dictionary on hydraulics as wedding gifts. Then friends from Tolya's and my classes brought smoked sausage, fish, and sardines. We danced and feasted until morning. This was on Friday. On Saturday, of course, the registry was closed. On Sunday, June 3, we departed in opposite directions for our summer internships. He went to Berezniki in the Ural Mountains, while I was sent to Armenia in the Caucasus. We set up a romantic meeting: August 15 at two in the afternoon at the railroad station of the New Afon, a lovely resort on the Black Sea.

Returning home in the fall, we were too lazy to register our marriage. So we signed the papers fifteen years later, just before filling out documents for emigration.

10 The First Day of My Honeymoon

At the beginning of August my internship ended. I boarded the Yerevan-Moscow train and set out for New Afon for our honeymoon. While sitting in my train compartment, a pock-marked Abkhazian man named Shota came on to me. He treated me to strawberries and cherries and hinted at his high social standing in Abkhazia, a province of Georgia. Upon discovering that I was a newlywed and there was no hope for love at first sight, he switched off his charm and we became friends.

"Listen, what are you going to New Afon for? What is there to see in New Afon? There is nothing but pure boredom and monks crawling all over the place. Normal people vacation in Sukhumi. Sukhumi is the capital where you can amuse yourself until dawn, and it is stocked just as well as Moscow. And I don't mean to brag, but Shota carries some weight there."

"I do believe you, Shota Georgeevich. Thank you very much, but there is no way I can stay in Sukhumi because my husband is coming to New Afon in two days, and I still need to find a room for us."

"You offend me . . . In Sukhumi you will not need to lift a finger. I'll fix you up like a queen so that no riffraff is around to bother you."

"But my husband will be waiting for me in *Afon*."

"Waiting, shmaiting. You keep repeating that like a parrot. I will tell him to continue on to Sukhumi, and he'll run to you with wings on his feet. You'll see. Just tell me where he is coming from and when."

"From Berezniki on the fifteenth of August. There will be a telegram for me in Afon."

"We will get the telegram in Sukhumi, and I will put you up in the Hotel Sinop. There is the beach, and sun, and palms, and waves. On my word, it is the picture of nature. When I make a promise, I keep my word. I am well known for this, and so far I have never let anyone down!" His pitch was so convincing that I got off with him in Sukhumi.

Two military personnel were waiting by the train car. They greeted Shota reverently. The four of us traversed the station building and walked up to a white Volga. In the car Shota transformed: he tensed every muscle, puffed his cheeks, stuck his chin up, squinted, and muttered through his teeth, "To the office for starters."

It was all of 200 meters to the "office." We drove up to the doors, and I saw a sign that read:

SUKHUMI RAILROAD BUREAU

OF THE COMMITTEE FOR STATE SECURITY

Shota cast a smug sideways glance at my pallid face. The memory of Captain Dyomin and his railroad KGB station was very much alive in me. We went up to the second floor, walked through gloomy narrow corridors, and stopped in front of a door covered in black leather. Shota Georgeevich flung it open before me. "Please come in and relax. Think of this as home."

With the gesture of a tired governor-general, he pointed me to an armchair, but seated himself on a table. Shota's office was much more luxurious than Dyomin's. Everything there, with the exception of mandatory portraits of Lenin, Dzerzhinski, and Khrushchev, was decorated in black leather—the sofa, the armchair, both telephones, the lamp, and even the inkstand. A black leather jacket hung from the coat rack. Shota produced a black leather cigarette case, drew out a French Gauloise cigarette, tapped it on the top of the case, flicked a black leather lighter (which played a melody from *The Barber of Seville*), and, threw himself into his chair, leaning back with a sweet smile. Next he picked up the phone and spoke to someone in the Abkhazian language. At that very moment the other phone rang. Shota lifted the receiver to his other ear without removing the cigarette from his mouth. It was a masterful pas de trois. He laughed into the first receiver and told someone off on the other one, roared into the first and cooed into the second. Then he laid down on the table the first receiver, from which quiet croaking noises could be heard. He probably was telling some anecdote into the second receiver because he chuckled to himself and then, rocking back in the chair, suddenly asked in Russian, "Do you understand the delicacy of the situation?"

Obviously, someone understood the delicacy at the other end, because Shota began to nod his head. "Think about it, my friend, such mistakes cost heads." Then he laid the second receiver on the table as well, and it continued to yelp next to the croaking one.

"This jerk Gargadze is a riot! Such a dolt . . . It's as if he weren't Georgian at all."

I had not the slightest idea who Gargadze was, but I asked politely, "What is it about Gargadze that does not please you?"

Shota did not respond. He stood up from behind the table, walked to the bookshelf, slipped his hand between the seventh and eighth volumes of Lenin's *Complete Collection of Works*, and produced two glasses and a bottle of Armenian cognac.

"I propose a toast to the beginning of your happy married life."

"Shota Georgeevich, you have forgotten to hang up the receivers, so your phones are always busy. Probably no one will be able to reach you."

"The phones are busy because the boss is busy . . ." He threw the first receiver onto its hook, and muttered something into the second one. Among incomprehensible guttural sounds I could make out the words "Afon" and "Dargis."

We drank up the cognac, and then the phone rang again. Shota listened to the report.

"There is a telegram for you: 'Will be in Afon the fifteenth on Moscow-Tbilisi express stop check arrival time on schedule stop missed you like crazy last days tender kisses your Tolya.'"

"Just how did you intercept such private correspondence, Shota Georgeevich?"

"Oh, don't be so naive," he said, waving his hand. "Better give me a brief description of your husband."

"In what way?"

"In a direct way. What does he look like?"

"I think he looks beautiful. But what does that matter to you?"

"I'm afraid that you are not too bright . . . Honey, we need to be able to recognize him so that we can meet him courteously and ask him to continue his trip to Sukhumi."

Tolya's verbal portrait was relayed right then and there to one of the receivers.

When we drove up to the Hotel Sinop, we saw the following sign:

ABSOLUTELY NO VACANCIES TILL END OF SEASON

The manager met us with a ceremonious bow and asked whether I preferred a room with a view of the Black Sea or of their "world-famous" rose garden. I said that I preferred a room that was less expensive. This answer seemed rather vulgar to my benefactors. Shota said that money shouldn't matter during a honeymoon.

"Money shouldn't matter *at all*," the manager echoed as he turned his bulging eyes toward the beautiful clouds, dreamily counting his millions. Then he led us through the hotel. I chose a magnificent room with two beds, two dressers, two chairs, and a sink. American barracks must look just like this. Shota himself brought my suitcase from his Volga and told me to rest until evening. He told me that at a quarter past seven he would pick me up and take me to dinner at the Esher Restaurant. Then, as they say in English novels, "weary from the long journey, without taking off my traveling dress I threw myself down on the bed and fell sound asleep."

At precisely quarter past seven someone knocked at the door. On the landing stood a strange gentleman with a bluish-black stubble on his face and a huge flat cap with a visor (nicknamed in Russian "The airfield" because of its size and shape). He held out his hand and solemnly said, "Ashot, fabric wear."

I asked what was that supposed to mean.

"Precisely what I said. I am in charge of Abkhazian fabric wear."

"And where is Shota Georgeevich?"

"He has been at the Esher since five o'clock. He had an unforeseen emergency. Official visitors from Tbilisi. He could not leave them. So he sent me to pick you up."

We got into the same white Volga and set out for the Esher. This restaurant was absolutely gorgeous. It was set in a grotto among mountain cliffs. A mountain stream babbled and meandered between the tables. Multicolored lights, hidden among moss-covered stones, illuminated the pebbles on the bottom and the shimmering trout swiming in the water reflecting soft patches of light onto the rhododendrons and laurel bushes. Stairs carved into the rock lead from the main hall to small private rooms. Ashot, the Fabric Man, led me into one of the private rooms. The table was set for three, and what a table! A feast of flavors and colors. In the center loomed a tower of marinated appetizers interwoven with fresh coriander and tarragon shoots. Fried lamb chops, a feta cheese pie called *khachapouri,* beans with walnuts, called *lobio;* and chicken in walnut sauce, called *satsivi* emitted an aroma of heavenly herbs. Bottles of cognac and wonderful Georgian wines sparkled among the dishes. The Fabric Man and I began to eat. In complete silence. We were separated from the main room by a heavy velvet curtain, and though I did not see what was happening there, voices, laughter, and the clinking of glasses could be heard. Then the music died down and chairs moved. The curtain was pushed aside and Shota popped into the room. Red curls twined around his head to form a halo; his freckled face was flushed and shiny. Shota was more than just tipsy.

"Eat. Don't be shy, and don't worry, and don't hurry," he said. "Soon I'll order some shish kebabs and chicken in pomegranate sauce . . . the best in Abkhazia and in the world. And as soon as my boss leaves, I will join you."

"Whom are you chattering with there, Shota?" A slender, gray-haired man, looking like an elegant lion, peered from behind the curtain. When he saw me, his eyes grew round.

"Just a high school friend, absolutely nothing interesting," Shota mumbled, forcing the gray-haired man back with his shoulder.

"Oh really? But I think this is very interesting indeed." The elegant lion stepped into the room. "This Ashot is also your school friend? What a strange sense of humor you have . . . Ashot, do you even know how to spell *school?*

Ashot stood at attention and did not dare to respond.

"And where is the young lady from? I've never seen her in your hen house before."

"She is the wife of a dear friend of mine who is a mathematical genius in Leningrad. He is arriving tomorrow."

"And just how will you be entertaining the young lady in the meantime? Quite admirably, I'm sure, but allow me to relieve you of this burden. May I dance with you?" He turned to me and, without waiting for a reply, added, "I will go and ask them to play a waltz."

The gray-haired man left. The Fabric Man still did not dare to move.

"That is Roman Berzeneshvili, the General Public Prosecutor of Georgia," Shota blurted out, "a womanizer and bootlicker. Don't even think of associating with him." He stuck his hand into his pocket, took out a revolver, and adroitly threw it into my lap. I completely froze from surprise and from the touch of cold metal and had just enough time to cover the revolver with the tablecloth before the prosecutor came back.

"May I?" he asked, extending both of his hands to me.

I glanced at Shota. He was looking dreamily into the distance somewhere above my head.

"Thank you, but I cannot. Besides, I don't know how . . ."

"Well, excuse me then . . ." The prosecutor frowned and left.

"You are such a valiant man, Shota Georgeevich," said the Fabric Man, the first to open his mouth.

"Nonsense. It's an old tested trick. A woman cannot dance with a weapon on her knees."

"But a woman can move the weapon from her lap onto the table," I said as my fear passed and I became angry.

"A proper woman—never! Judge for yourself; just use your head. If they see that I throw revolvers around, they will fire me and then prevent me from finding any future employment. Not to mention that I would have to serve time—no less than five years. A proper woman with high moral principles would never do such a thing. I know, being myself something of a psychologist. Give me back my toy now. My pocket feels empty without it."

"Take it yourself. I'm afraid even to touch it."

"Oh, it doesn't bite, though it does shoot . . . but not at everyone." Having chuckled at his own wit, Shota hid the revolver in his pocket and looked around the table. "Is there enough of everything? Or should I order something more?" At that, he disappeared.

The evening dragged on endlessly. The Fabric Man drank cognac and became more and more depressing. He looked as if he had just buried his family. At last I asked him to take me back to Sinop.

"Shota Georgeevich did not give such an order."

The music in the main hall died down, feet began to shuffle, voices quieted. The ball was over, yet Shota did not show up.

"Do you plan to keep me here all night?"

"I do not know." The Fabric Man's face expressed his confusion. "On the one hand, I was ordered to guard and entertain you, but on the other, I was not told until what time. And what if he has some plans for you?"

"What are you talking about? Take me home right this instant or else!"

We left the restaurant. It was muggy out. Stars shone in a black sky, in the bushes cicadas jingled, and the air was drunk with the aroma of sweet-smelling flowers. In the parking lot there were no cars other than our Volga.

"What plans does Shota Georgeevich have for me?"

"Various ones. Who knows. Perhaps a rest in his cottage, for example," he replied, waving his hand toward the side of the invisible mountains. We had not yet driven off when we were blinded by headlights, and from the pitch darkness a military vehicle emerged with Shota at the wheel.

"How wonderful and fortunate that I caught you. Don't be offended; business is business. I will drive you to Sinop myself. And you, Ashot, park that heap in the garage."

"In which cottage are you resting, Shota Georgeevich?"

"Me? Resting? Who told you such nonsense? Ashot told you such nonsense? Ashot, you are a barbarian of poor cultural upbringing. Because of you I am ashamed to be an Abkhazian."

After we arrived at the hotel, Shota leapt out of the car, ran around it, helped me out, escorted me to the door, and on parting kissed my hand—thus demonstrating his very high cultural upbringing.

"Be ready at four o'clock tomorrow afternoon. We'll drive to the station to meet your husband. On the way we'll drop by the Botanical Garden, for I've ordered them to cut some roses."

The Moscow-Tbilisi express train pulled into the New Afon station. Tolya had left his compartment and was standing in the corridor with his suitcases. As the train car lurched forward and then froze, several armed soldiers jumped into it from each end and moved toward each other, shouting, "Dargis! Anatoly Dargis!"

"I am Dargis," Tolya breathed out with his lips pale with terror.

As the soldiers clustered around him, firmly blocking the exit, a lieutenant of the KGB flashed his service identification in front of Tolya's face. "You have been ordered to continue your trip to Sukhumi," he said.

"Why? What happened?" Tolya made an attempt to step forward but ran into a human wall.

"Mr. Dargis, obey orders, or we will have to use force. That would not be in your best interest."

"Just a minute! My wife is meeting me here! She is somewhere on the platform, I must notify her!"

"You must obey orders, and our orders are to not let you off in Afon."

"Well, may I at least shout out to her?"

"I'll show you how to shout! Shut up!" yelled the lieutenant, losing his temper.

The train started moving. Under this military escort, Anatoly Dargis continued his journey. He was jostled into his compartment, where several soldiers kept him under constant surveillance.

"Express train number 17, Moscow-Tbilisi, is arriving in Sukhumi, the capital of sunny Abkhazia," the loudspeaker wheezed.

Barely managing the prickly handful of roses, I dashed along the train cars. Shota trotted along behind. Two soldiers jumped down from the steps of car number 5 and stood by both sides of the door. Behind them an officer descended, saluted to Shota, and reported that the mission had been accomplished. Then the remaining military personnel poured out of the car, and at last Tolya appeared in the doorway.

"Hi, my love," I shouted. "You see how splendidly everything turned out?"

He stood, not moving, and looked at me like a cornered wild beast.

"Come on out, you are here at last!"

Tolya slowly descended the steps of the car. Behind him a porter was carrying his luggage.

"Hello, darling! Hi, honey! Welcome!" I held out the roses.

"Is this all your doing?" Tolya asked in a colorless voice.

"Of course, who else? Instead of dragging myself through Afon, I . . ."

Tolya drew back his arm and slapped me in the face with such force that I saw stars and I heard the Tzar Bell booming in my head. The platform was covered with freshly cut roses, but I somehow managed to stay standing. The soldiers ran up to Tolya and twisted his arms behind his back.

"As you were!" yelped Shota Georgeevich. "Don't hold this bandit! We do not engage in criminal affairs! Solonidze! Buridze, call the police! It's their business! Such educated people, acting like hooligans!"

And thus began my honeymoon with Tolya Dargis.

11 A Seaport in Constantinople

On our border with Turkey, or is it Pakistan,
There is a neutral zone, to the right, where there are bushes,
 Our border guards are standing with their captain,
 And on the left are the other side's lookouts.
But in the neutral zone there are flowers
Of unspeakable beauty . . .

Vladimir Vysotsky*
"In the Neutral Zone"

Our daughter, Katya Dargis, was born in Finland, four feet from the Soviet border. I neither intended to cross this border nor was I thinking of guarding it. Instead, I had tried to complete a "top-secret government mission" there. After I graduated from the Mining Institute as a hydrogeologist, I was hired by the Leningrad Water Works and prepared to begin work on September 1. All summer I was extremely nervous, seeing as how I was irreversibly pregnant and knowing that young pregnant specialists bring out strong feelings of hatred in their supervisors. In those days, pregnant women were entitled to four months of paid leave, two months before the birth of the baby and two after it. Moreover, according to the law, they had a right to a whole year of unpaid leave, and the company could not fire

---

*Vladimir Vysotsky was an extremely popular actor, singer, and writer of unofficial songs. "In the Neutral Zone" was written in 1964.

them. Thus the pregnant professionals undermined state plans, budgets, and, in general, the basis of the socialist structure. These rules applied to field geologists as well. Not wishing to traumatize my boss on my first day of work, I sewed up a garment that was meant to conceal my barrel-shaped figure. Mother dubbed this dress "la trois-quarts," and so attired, I showed up at work. The manager, Kira Vasilyeva, bored through me like a drill, and with spite in her eyes spat out, "When is the baby due?"

"Whose baby are we talking about?"

"Certainly not mine." Her sarcasm had no limit.

"There is no cause to worry for at least another three and a half years."

"In my opinion, three months, no more. Just what was Perepelkin thinking when he hired you? You of course must understand what a strain you are placing on the department's budget. Therefore, as long as you can move under your own power, there will be absolutely no exceptions. Starting Monday . . . into the field!"

"I do not handle the heat very well."

"Neither do I. But, as you put it, there is no cause to worry. Heat is not on the agenda. You are assigned to the hydrogeological group that will be working near the Finnish border. Keep this confidential and brief yourself on the documentation. This is a government project. You will find underground drinking water there, or not a stone of this department will be left standing."

Now picture gray storm clouds above you. It is drizzling. You are in a pine forest. Moss and heather are under your feet, and you are surrounded by granite boulders of the glacial period. In the distance a woodpecker is hammering away monotonously. You are in the gloomy north, or, rather, on the border between Russia and Finland, a godforsaken place. Captain Tapochkin is the commander at the border post, where his wife, Tosya, languishes from idleness and boredom and where thirty-four big men watch over the security of the Soviet border.

After the death of Comrade Stalin, the last of the Four (who was demented and paranoid), a new leader, Comrade Khrushchev (who was friendly and eccentric but had not yet become the Fifth), opened the window to the western world while pounding the lectern in the UN with his shoe. He established economic, cultural, and personal connections with the West, but he was not content with that. Gesturing royally, he opened the door to international tourism and invited our neighbors to travel to our country without any hesitation, or constraints, simply as guests. He went to such liberal lengths that he was even thinking of letting his own citizens travel to nearby countries. And, in order to make the hitherto unprecedented freedoms official, he signed an agreement with Finland on the extradition of political refugees. However, after various celebrations and exchanges of folk singers and dance ensembles between the two countries, he changed his mind about spoiling his citizens any longer. To hell with them—they have enough firsthand experience with the West from the Baltic republics. After all, store signs there are written in Latin letters rather than Cyrillic.

Not so long ago our border-guards listened for the footsteps of foreign spies, but now, *voila,* motley groups of imported tourists poured over our border. Every Friday the newly paved concrete roads were opened to buses, Volkswagens, Renaults, and Peugeots carrying Finns in highly valued jeans. On Sundays the guests went back, their suitcases bursting with bottles of Stolichnaya, balalaikas, and cans of smoky-black caviar, which they got in exchange for their dungarees. Our modest border post has turned into the hospitable gates of Great Power, staffed by the Border Patrol.

The reliable trained dogs used for guarding the frontier were moved further back into the woods. They were replaced at the border by smart-looking customs officials and interpreters. Captain Tapochkin personally memorized twenty-nine words in English and eleven in some Finno-Ugric tongue, and his wife, Tosya, mastered the words *bonjour* and *au revoir.*

After checking their documents and searching their luggage, the customs officials gallantly greeted the tourists and wished them a happy weekend. However, the tourists sometimes ran into patches of thorns. Sometimes they wanted to walk around, stretch their legs, and—pardon the rudeness—use the toilet. In order to reveal the underlying cause of an international scandal, I must describe the architecture of this facility.

The washroom at the guarded point of entry was nothing more than a two-seater wooden outhouse. Once international tourism was allowed, the authorities renewed the plywood partitions, washed the obscene graffiti and sexually explicit pictures from the walls, and painted the English letters *M* and *W* on the doors. But purple flies buzzed inside and out just as before, sounding like war planes, which caused the spoiled foreigners to go into a state of nervous shock. To modernize this establishment, the authorities ordered two porcelain toilets from Moscow and installed them over the infamous holes. They posted a soldier with buckets of water at the entrance to the outhouse. His assignment was to pour water into the toilet bowls after a tourist exited. On busy days two soldiers were on duty. One kept constant vigil around the *M* and *W,* while the other ran to the well and returned with buckets full of water. It seemed like the situation was under control.

But citizens of the great country are only human, and one day the soldier, Taifudinov, fell asleep at his post. And he dreamed of . . . Actually, what difference does that make? If he had told his dream to the war tribunal, it would have done nothing to soften their hearts. Taifudinov fell asleep and slept through his patriotic duty. He didn't check the toilet after it had been visited by the professor of sociology, and he let Renata Karelyainen, who was a singer in a nightclub, slip in unnoticed. She flew right back out. The lady turned out to be quite malicious. The marvelous palaces, museums, fountains, children's nurseries and kindergartens, and even tickets to the great ballet *Swan Lake* could not assuage her outrage over the pastoral customs of our great land. Upon returning to her country, which is barely noticeable on the world map, she sent an article to a newspaper with an unpronounceable title and also wrote a letter directly to Mr. Khrushchev.

"What a shame! What a disgrace! This is an outrage!" yelled the addressee, the leader of the great power. "Within two weeks we must build a new customs building with every . . . what is that word . . . *comfort.* But first, show me all the drawings!"

Three ministers—the Minister of the Water Works, the Minister of Geology, and the Minister . . . that is, the head of the KGB—stood at attention, not daring to move, and only when the great leader had burst out of the office in a rage did they muster enough courage to pass around a bottle of Valium. That same day, five architectural institutes, along with my Water Works, received a top priority, top secret, top government assignment: to erect *a new customs building with all the comforts.*

A week later five plans were laid out before Khrushchev. One building looked like a classic Greek temple; the second, like a Swiss chalet; the third, a glass pyramid, just like the new entrance to the Louvre; the fourth, like a fortress with embrasures for windows; and, from our Water Works, a Moorish palace, a miniature of the one in Constantinople.

Now picture yourself in Turkey, in Constantinople, in the suburb of Kasim-Pasha, by the small inner bay of the Golden Horn. The sky is piercing blue, the water is warm and of ever-changing colors, from malachite to pearly-opal to turquoise. Above your head sea gulls spread their wings;

around you is a well-dressed crowd speaking Turkish and Greek; and before your eyes stands a gracious building of Moorish architecture, straight from the pages of *A Thousand and One Nights,* almost as magnificent as the mosque of Bayazelt the First or the Palace of Alhambra in Granada.

"It is a beauty, it will do very well, it . . . just build it!" cried the Head of State.

Our group had won the contest. This beautiful miniature palace was built. It shone softly and elegantly among pine trees that looked like rose-colored ship masts. But, in all the hubbub of construction, they forgot about running water.

Feeling my daughter kicking and turning, I began my career in hydro-geological surveying. The first well dried up just as soon as we lowered the electric pump. Then the drunken superintendent, Boris, smashed that pump for its uselessness. We called for an oil rig brigade and drilled seven more shafts, but whatever water there was flowed into the cracks in the granite, and our shafts still remained dry. In the hope of finding a spring, I took a walk through the bluish, mossy, fairy-tale forest. Two border guards with German shepherds escorted me at a distance of ten feet. Suddenly I heard faraway the sound I had been waiting for—the sound of a water stream. Forgetting about the guards, I tore ahead over tree stumps and fallen trees. Convinced that I was fleeing across the border, the guards chased after me with their dogs. The pursuit was not a long one. I fell, choking and screaming. The last thing I remember was the snarling canine jaws above me. I went into labor.

The bubbling sound was not a hallucination. *I had found water!* My efforts, however, were in vain. The stream ran from a lake in Finland, which, though friendly, was still a capitalist country. Therefore, the enemies and secret agents had ample opportunity to sprinkle arsenic or uranium into the crystal stream. Instructions were posted about this: "It is strictly forbidden to use any running water for consumption or in the plumbing system if the source of it is located outside the state border of the Soviet Union."

The law is the law; there is no getting around it. Years passed. My daughter grew up and graduated from high school. And on the Soviet-Finnish border, in the Moorish building, by the doors labeled *M* and *W,* guards still stand vigil with their buckets of water. They uphold the sanitary reputation of the miniature version of the castle in Constantinople.

12 Gainsborough's *Blue Boy*

Insomnia has been the curse of my life since my youth. For years I've been sleeping no more than four–five hours a day. But once we had handed in our documents for emigration, I stopped sleeping altogether. For four months, I took all imaginable kinds of sleeping pills without any results. During the day I walked and talked like a zombie. I lost thirty pounds and developed blue circles under my eyes. My head was shaking and my hands trembling.

Finally, two pieces of paper arrived in a mail: a permission to emigrate and an order to leave the country within ten working days.

So, just ten days remained until our departure. Tolya still had not recovered from his mysterious illness of high fever with no other symptoms and moved about with difficulty. Katya barricaded herself from the outside world and devoted herself to the study of Italian language; right before we left, she was reading Dante in the original. Mama lay with a hot water bottle on her head and a nitroglycerin tablet under her tongue, staring blankly at our beautiful antique furniture, the Limoges dinner set, paintings, and books from our unique library of poetry, which my parents had been collecting for half a century. We were allowed to take only two pieces of luggage per person with us. Some distinguished people scooped up our treasures for a song. Taking the advice of more experienced people, we put our emergency money into icons, which these same experienced people promised to carry across the Soviet-Hungarian border so that we could live happily ever after on foreign soil.

We have been living on foreign soil for fifteen years now, but to this day we have found neither those icons nor those people.

From sunrise to sunset, I spent my time running to various mysterious Soviet establishments to obtain the most absurd certificates to prove that we didn't owe anything to anybody. I had to go to a vacuum cleaner rental store, the state auto inspection station, Leningrad Gas, Leningrad Energy, the Russian Museum, and the local Party committee. Franz Kafka should have been born in Russia.

One day I returned home to find Mother having a nervous breakdown. She was sobbing, holding to her chest a silver-plated sugar bowl and a small bronze bell, which had been in our family through three revolutions and two world wars.

"I am not going *anywhere* without them, I will not budge from this place. I'd sooner kill myself," she repeated in a monotone.

"Mum, throw that junk out. I'll have to get another certificate to get them out of the country. To hell with it, with this sugar bowl . . ."

"I am not going. I will not leave these things. I cannot," Mother proclaimed. Her grieving voice and tear-streaked face wrenched my heart. I took the sugar bowl and the small bell from her hands and dashed off to Nevsky Prospect, to the Department of Culture. On the door to Comrade Nosova's office hung a list of objects forbidden from leaving the Soviet Union. I knocked and, without waiting for an answer, flew into the office. Comrade Nosova was talking on the phone. When she saw me she covered the receiver with her hand and pointed to the door with her chin. I walked up to her desk.

"Do not be shy with her. Be firm. No exceptions . . ." She droned into the receiver. "So what if she is a star, and so what if they will make a fuss. I don't give a shit . . ."

It later became clear that the conversation was about Elizabeth Taylor, who was starring in the Soviet-American film *Blue Bird*. During her stay in Leningrad, Liz had bought a malachite table from speculators, and the customs official did not know whether to let it through. Comrade Nosova did not advise doing so.

Having finished with Elizabeth Taylor, Nosova took up with me.

"We do not handle estimates today. Go and sign up with the secretary for Thursday."

"I am not leaving until you write a certificate authorizing me to take these things," I said, and put the sugar bowl and the bell on her table. Nosova was dumfounded.

"This is all that you have?"

"This is all that I want to take with me."

Her face expressed bewilderment at the worthlessness of the objects, but she quickly took charge.

"That is absolutely impossible; it is absolutely forbidden."

"Why?"

"Because."

"Where is it written?"

"In the instructions."

"Please, show me the instructions."

"I will not. I am not required to."

"Show me the instructions this very moment."

"Get the hell out of here or else I'll call the police!"

"What is all this about?" I burst out. "Are there any laws at all in our country?"

"There are no laws in our country!" Nosova screamed.

My rage evaporated instantly, like a drop of water on a hot skillet.

"Aha, very interesting . . . In our country there are no laws? Did I hear you correctly? You must agree, that is a pretty unusual statement, and I hope in the future you will not deny saying it . . . Please turn on your radio tomorrow. You will hear it on the BBC."

"That is not fair," she whimpered like an old woman. "People say all kinds of things in the heat of the moment."

"Yes, it happens," I sympathized. "I propose that you show me the instructions in which it says that the sugar bowl and the bell are forbidden items that can't be taken out of the U.S.S.R."

In response, Nosova grabbed the receiver and said softly, "Yuri Ivanovich, come in for a moment."

Into the office walked a man shaped like a refrigerator. His eyes were not visible through the thick lenses, which reflected the table lamp.

"This one here," Nosova said, pointing at me, "is demanding instructions on what is not allowed to be taken out."

"But everything is forbidden," Yuri Ivanovich replied lightly.

"Show me, please, the instructions."

"What other instructions do you need? The list is nailed to the door there; it said in plain Russian: works of art, bronze, silver, old samovars . . ."

"But silver-plated sugar bowls?" I interjected. "This one, for example," and I held out the sugar bowl and the bell to him.

"But this is absolutely forbidden."

"Why?"

"Because." Turning to Nosova, he said firmly, "And you, Galina Andreevna, don't get worked up over this shit. It is written law."

"But in our country, as I've just learned, there are no laws."

"What? What did you say?" Yuri Ivanovich asked jovially, his eyes glimmering in anticipation of a juicy confrontation.

"Never mind, never mind. We will handle this," Nosova quickly mumbled as she came out from behind the desk and escorted her boss to the door. Then she exhaled and said in a quite human voice: "It was stupid of me to call him in here. Now this does not depend on me. You will have to go to Moscow, to the Ministry of Culture. Do not worry: I will call the director now and ask that you be seen from three to five tomorrow."

The next day, first person I met in the corridor of the Ministry of Culture was my old friend, the artist Erik Melenin. He was leaning against the dark brown wall and studying the color of his boot.

"Erik, darling! Are you emigrating as well?"

"Where did you get that idea? I just got here . . . I arrived from the country last night. I think I'll stay a while in Moscow."

"But what are you doing at the ministry?"

"I have an appointment. We are organizing a new exhibit of nonconformist artists, and I came to get permission for it . . . And, while I'm here, I might as well order bulldozers and a wrecking ball so the minister of our culture can destroy our paintings more efficiently."

Erik Melenin was famous for his macabre humor.

We embraced and kissed good-bye, thinking that we were parting forever though, as it turned out, it was not for long at all. Six months later Erik and his wife, without a drop of Jewish blood in them, were kicked out of the country to go to Israel but instead landed in France.

A tall gray-haired woman with a pseudo-intellectual face took me into her office. She extended her hand and invited me to have a seat. I placed the sugar bowl and bell on the table. The woman looked over my treasures and sighed with pity.

"I am afraid I am going to have to upset you. I cannot give you any kind of certificate. You see, I am a specialist in pre-nineteenth-century art objects, but these are *utensils,* without question, of a later period. You must go to the commission at the Tretyakov Gallery. The commission operates on Tuesdays in the Novodevichy Cloister, but I would strongly advise you to make an appointment ahead of time."

"You . . . you, I hope, are joking?"

"Unfortunately, I have no time to joke while at work."

"But these are not art objects or even utensils. This is junk, family relics."

"I do believe you. Nevertheless . . . please, do not think that these laws were written by me. These are policies of all civilized countries. Take England, for example. Remember the international scandal which broke out over Gainsborough's *Blue Boy*. An English family wanted to take this masterpiece dating from the late 1860s to the early 1870s out of Great Britain—this painting was a family heirloom to them as well—and the English government would not allow it. The Queen herself signed the order. So, there is nothing more that can be done."

"But my sugar bowl was not created by Gainsborough, Titian, or even Picasso!"

"That does not prevent it from having artistic value."

"Then buy it from me. Buy it and put it in the Hermitage."

"We have no need for it," said the woman, looking at her watch. "Excuse me. I have no more time. We already have been talking for fifteen minutes." She got up from behind the table, indicating that my session with her was over.

An hour later I entered the wing of the Novodevichy Cloister. A militiaman was keeping watch by the door with a sign, "Commission for the Appraisal of Art Objects."

"Your ticket, citizen."

"What ticket?"

"Are you registered?"

"I will only be a minute."

"Vacate the vestibule," the militiaman ordered in a booming voice as he blocked the door to the Commission for the Appraisal of Art Objects.

I had no more strength left to fight. I returned to Leningrad, and while packing our suitcases I simply threw in the sugar bowl and the small bell. The customs official did not pay the slightest attention to our treasures as he went through our luggage.

I honestly do not know what the English family resorted to in order to take their family heirloom out of Great Britain. Last summer I saw with my own eyes Gainsborough's portrait of Jonathan Battle, known as the *Blue Boy,* at the Huntington Library in Pasadena, California.

13 The Leather Connection

And so we arrived in Boston, in the Commonwealth of Massachusetts. During the four months of our journey we were overwhelmed by our first glimpses of the capitalist world. We left behind Vienna and the crowded, filthy hotel "zum Turken," where the owner, Frau Bettina, watched over the emigrants to make sure that they didn't use the gas stove more than once a day. We left behind Rome with its roasted chestnuts at Piazza del Poppolo, the Mercato Rotondo, where we shopped for turkey wings (50 cents a pound), and the flea market Americana where we sold Russian souvenirs for a whistle. Then came New York, horrifying and glorious, the South Bronx with its high rises gutted by fire and with their windows smashed, looking like Stalingrad in 1943.

Left behind were the days when we were deaf and dumb foreigners taking our first steps in the new land—the sound of my voice speaking broken English, my encounter with our landlady who said, "If you don't like my roaches, go back to Russia." Ahead lay still more bouts of culture shock, nostalgia, sadness, hope, joy, worries, new friendships, and endless attempts to find a professional job . . .

The best part of me is my curriculum vitae. I have an impressive Ph.D. in geology from the Leningrad University. I specialized in weak soils, more precisely, in the microstructure of clay. I hold the distinguished honor of being the only woman among 495 male graduates. I was voted Clay Queen by my professors and colleagues, and my year book predicted that I was the most likely to win the Nobel Prize.

But in Boston, I became unemployed and, I am afraid, unemployable. I searched through the Help Wanted sections of the Boston papers day after day but did not see one ad calling for my skills and experience. Each time I visited an employment agency, the staff would come out to see for themselves a woman geologist. The trouble was that despite all my personal charm and qualifications, they simply had no job for me.

Back home in Leningrad I would have known precisely how to get an unavailable job—whom to send flowers to, whom to invite to dinner, whom to charm, and whom to bribe. Here, I found myself in a vacuum.

A friend of mine, a former art critic in the Soviet Union and now a cab driver in New York City, told me, "Those wonderful methods don't work for us foreigners. Where can we, for God's sake, find those connections? Who needs our splendid Soviet academic degrees and our lousy English? Throw out your golden Ph.D. and look for a real job."

Was my English really *that* lousy? It is hard to tell because Americans are very tolerant. When I knew four phrases—"Please," "Thank you," "How much?" and "How are you?"—everybody said "Your English is spectacular." After I had learned ten more sentences, they would say, "Your English is very good." I became extremely proud of myself until this same art critic/cab driver friend burst my bubble: "Don't be so naive. When no one comments about your English, then you will know that you are in business." Finally I gave up, framed my diplomas, put them on the bathroom wall, and applied to McDonald's. Unfortunately, I was too old for Ronald. Kentucky Fried Chicken had long waiting lists. Nannys, Inc. was afraid I would inject Communist ideology into American babies. Nursing Homes, Inc. did not trust my ability to clean their floors.

One day, while wandering through Brookline, I passed by a store called Leather Land. I had always loved the touch and the smell of fine leather but never had enough money to match my fancy taste. Gazing through the window, I noticed a sign, "Salesperson Wanted." I pushed open the glass door. Chimes rang melodically as I stepped onto a fluffy emerald-colored rug. Zebra skins, bear heads, and deer noses covered the store walls. As I took a few more steps, brass floor lamps with opal shades bent to greet me. They cast their warm light on crocodile skin briefcases, snakeskin pocketbooks, suede purses, and alligator wallets. How many reptiles and other members of the amphibian family had to give their lives to keep this elegant store in business? The pungent odor of leather goods mixed with a wave of Balenciaga perfume intimidated me and made me feel out of place.

A handsome gray-haired gentleman, with the manners of a European prime minister, rose to greet me and asked if he could help me. I pointed to the sign in the window.

"Are you looking for a job?" he asked, smiling.

"Thank you, yes. Very much."

"Would you sit down please?" He motioned to a large deep leather chair. "My name is Arthur Kempler." I introduced myself and he asked, "Where are you from, and how do you like America?"

"I from Russia. I am in love to be here."

"Do you have any experience selling leather goods?"

"Not sure. No, not think so." I stuttered trying to smile charmingly.

"Okay. Let me put it this way. When was the last time you sold a brief-case?"

"I never don't." Squirming and ashamed of my English, I explained to him, "No briefcases. No suitcases. I never sold nothing in my whole life at all. I don't know how to do."

Prime Minister Kempler smiled gently. "Then I'm afraid I can't help you. Sorry."

I also mumbled "Sorry" and headed for the door.

"Wait," said Mr. Kempler. "Wait a minute. Is there anything you know how to do?"

Dropping my eyes, I admitted that I had a Ph.D. in geology. His formal manners disappeared as he slapped his knee, exclaiming, "No kidding? What a riot! Isn't that amazing? Believe it or not, my son David is a geologist, too. I always dreamt he would take over Leather Land, but he hates this business. Instead he became a professor at MIT. You know where that is? Just across the river."

Overwhelmed by such a coincidence, Mr. Kempler picked up the phone and called his son. Unfortunately, I did not understand a word he said. Then he turned to me. "Go to MIT right away. Go to my boy. He will be waiting for you."

On the subway to Cambridge, I rehearsed my first sentence to Professor Kempler. Then, I would give him my résumé and proudly would remain silent.

David Kempler sat in an old oak chair. He was dressed in patched hiking shorts and a red T-shirt preaching BE KIND TO AMPHIBIANS AND REPTILES. His long legs were resting atop his desk, holding down a pile of papers. A bush of rusty, wild hair matched his beard and created the impression of an abandoned and abused Scotch terrier. I was asked to be seated and immediately heard the familiar questions, "Where are you from, and how do you like America?" David poured me a cup of coffee and showed me a picture of his wife, two sons, a poodle, and a pair of Siamese cats. I expressed my admiration for his family. Then I did my best to explain who I was and my specific expertise.

"What a shame. Unfortunately, I never dealt with weak soils," he said. "Moreover, I flunked all those courses in college. But there must be someone who knows something about it." He closed his eyes and thought. "Wait!" He jumped up. "Bert! Of course, Bert!"

David picked up the phone and spoke to this mysterious "Bert," but once again the conversation was far above my head. Then he drew me a map of the MIT campus and marked a cross at Bert's office. His directions included Bert's real name—Professor Herbert Einstein. I was thrilled. At least I could show that I was familiar with scientific giant's name. "Is he related to . . . ?"

David Kempler nodded casually. "Sure. Bert is the grandson of old Albert."

For me, a meeting with the grandson of "old Albert" was like dancing with Madonna would be for an American teenage boy. My limbs shook with each step closer to Bert's office. I had to hold on to the walls to steady my nerves. Professor Einstein was a striking man, about forty. He greeted me on the threshold of his office and—guess what?—immediately offered me a cup of coffee. He spoke with a pronounced German accent. To my relief, he did not ask any of the traditional questions that constantly fall on an émigré's head. Professor Einstein obviously did not care where I was from or how I liked America. Our conversation lasted no more than ten minutes. After looking over my résumé, he said, "Here is a list of companies you might try. Start with Rock, Clay, etc. The president, Sal Scardetti, is an old friend of mine. I will call him about you after lunch. Please leave your home number." Professor Einstein shook my hand and saw me to the door.

As soon as I got home, the phone rang. I looked at it with disgust. As much as I adored that sound in Leningrad, I detested it now because each ring meant linguistic torture. Unfortunately, Americans still do not speak Russian, and my telephone English was a sheer disaster. Once I confessed my phonophobia to my upstairs neighbor. She tried to reassure me. The poor naive soul picked up the telephone receiver and showed me how harmless it was. "You see, my dear, the voltage does not hurt at all. You just have to say hello and listen for the answer. Everyone in this country knows how to use it, and I am quite sure that someday you will have it in Russia, too." Then she reached into her apron pocket and, pulling out a crescent-shaped yellow object, proceeded to instruct me. "This is a fruit. It is called a banana. It grows where the weather is warm. It is very delicious. Try it, but please remember to take off the skin. Otherwise, your stomach will ache." After this lecture, she left.

So, I stared at the ringing phone and peeled the yellow crescent. After five rings, I took a deep breath, lifted the receiver, and said "Hello."

"Hello. This is Salvatore Scardetti from Rock, Clay, etc." He spoke so slowly and clearly that even the most illiterate orangutan would have understood. "I would like you to come for an interview." His next words were his address, which of course I did not understand.

"When?"

"Right away."

"Where?"

He repeated the address.

"Big problem." I said. "No car."

"Rent one, please. We will pay."

"Don't know how."

"Okay, take a taxi." He laughed. "I'll expect you in an hour."

Easy to say, I thought. I ran upstairs to my "Banana Godmother," trying to solve three problems at once. First, I had no clothes for a formal interview. Second, I still didn't understand the address of the company. Finally, I had no taxi fare.

She also had trouble with my first problem. Her wardrobe was five sizes larger than mine. The second problem was easier. She took out the Yellow Pages and wrote down the name of the company and the address. She also gave me twenty dollars and called a taxi.

Ten minutes later, I was getting into the cab in my Hadassah Thrift Shop treasures—pink pants and an overblouse, which were in vogue in Florida in the early fifties. The cab driver was a huge black fellow with a deep scar on his left cheek. He scared me to death. As soon as the cab door was shut, I squeezed myself down in the back seat, trying to become invisible.

I was completely at his mercy. Who knew where I would wind up? He asked, "Where to, lady?" I handed him my neighbor's note.

"Oh, I heard of them. That's a big company. What are you going to do there?"

"Interview."

He clicked his tongue and shook his head. "I bet you're real nervous. But don't show 'em you're sweatin'. Be cool, honey, splash on some more perfume, and cross your legs real pretty, and them suckers will be in your hands real quick. You're not a bad looker, you know. I hope ya get the job."

When we arrived, I gave him the twenty dollar bill, but he raised his palm. "No, lady, the ride's on me. Go get 'em. Good luck, and God bless you!"

An angelic secretary greeted me like a long-lost sister and, with a dazzling smile, escorted me to the president's office. There was Salvatore Scardetti himself, olive skin, curly hair, puffy cheeks, plaid pants, and green shirt.

"Please sit down. Would you like a cup of coffee?" I did not dare to refuse even though it was the fifth one of the day.

"It looks like this is your lucky day. We have an opening. Our geologist just quit. He traded us for a pile of cold dead fish." My eyes popped out and he explained that their geologist had just bought a fish market in Maine. Then I heard: "Where are you from? How do you like America?"

The real interview began. I remember his questions, but I don't remember my answers. If I were in his place I would have suggested that I take up basket weaving. But to my surprise, Salvatore Scardetti said, "Not bad. Not bad at all. We will get back to you in a few days."

At the door, the "angel" gave me a forty-dollar check and whispered, "This is for your transportation expenses." I was speechless.

Three days later, I received a letter on fancy stationery: "We are happy to inform you . . . [yada, yada, yada] . . . with annual salary of $38,000." I was ready to call them to point out their typographical error. Surely there was a misplaced comma. There was no way it could be that much money. But it was.

My first working day turned out to be so disastrous that I was sure it would be my last. When I arrived in the morning, much to my delight I saw a big sign on the door: "A Russian is coming, a Russian is here. Welcome."

God, was I nervous. Everyone asked me, "How do you like America?" and "Would you like a cup of coffee?" By noon, though my kidneys were floating, I felt a little more at ease. People still smoked at the lab in those days, so I also dared to have a cigarette. I lit one and threw the match into the wastebasket. In a second the basket was ablaze like the Olympic torch. The flames engulfed two desks. Alarms rang. Sirens screeched. Three hook-and-ladder trucks and two ambulances arrived. Firemen, policemen, and paramedics yelled orders. Soot flew in the air. Water splashed everywhere.

Back home in my beloved country, I would certainly have been sent to jail for a good five years. But here, nobody blamed me. Nobody even looked in my direction. I hid in the ladies' room, half dead with fear, guilt, and regret that I had not fallen into the Atlantic Ocean on my way to these shores.

Two hours later, our lab was clean and quiet again. I had almost put my-self back together when the intercom broadcasted the cheerful voice of Mr. Scardetti: "May I have your attention, please? We have in our company a very charming but extremely clumsy Russian lady. She almost burned us all to smithereens. But thanks to you, my good staff, she didn't succeed. I commend you."

Yesterday was a very special day. It was my first anniversary at Rock, Clay, etc. Tomorrow I am off to Switzerland on my very first business trip. I am all set except for a new suitcase. Guess where I went? Right; I headed di-rectly for Leather Land. The door was ajar. Leather Land was even more glamorous than I had remembered it—lavish wall-to-wall leather and that wonderful aroma of Balenciaga. Fairy godfather Kempler did not recog-nize me. I handed him my business card. He stared at me for a second, then laughed and hugged me tight. "Now tell me, how can I help you?"

"I need a good traveling bag, not too expensive of course."

"Take you pick. For you, 30 percent off."

Oh, America the beautiful! The land of leather, the land of connections.

14 The End of Indian Summer

It was Indian summer in October. The leaves were almost ready to let go of their branches but were still stubbornly holding on, painting the landscape crimson and purple. The sky had already lost its piercing-blue color and had become pale, but the moss was still fresh. In it hid the last mushrooms of the year. The crickets and the birds were rejoicing, but aside from them and me, there was not a friendly soul in the forest. I listened to their voices and waited with a sinking heart, because in this peaceful world the war cry of the Simpson tribe could break out at any time.

Ecological problems had taken me to this part of New England. A chemical plant was to be built on the border of the Indian reservation in Mashpee on Cape Cod, Massachusetts. The plant was barely on paper, but demonstrations protesting pollution of the environment were already taking place. My assignment as a geologist was to prove that sewage from the future plant would not pollute this pristine region. I was to take samples of water from the rivers, streams, lakes, and ponds in order to determine their chemical composition.

"Be careful," the head geologist, Alan Hayward, said before I left. "The Indians started the battle to obtain neighboring lands for their reservation. At one time this land belonged to their ancestors. Of course, they are carrying on the battle legally; they are hiring lawyers, and so on, but . . . People are people, and sometimes they become aggressive. So don't roam about there at night alone."

This warning spoiled my mood instantly. I even called the Mashpee Town Hall: "Tell me, please, is it safe to work in your forests?"

"What are you talking about?" They were indignant. "Of course it is safe. In any case, safer than in New York City or Los Angeles. This blasted press whips up all kind of gossip! Come and see for yourself!" A long pause followed, then the town clerk said with what seemed like trepidation: "True, we have the unpredictable Simpson brothers, mischievous kids. Anything can be expected from them. But we will have a talk with them. Do not worry."

And so, practically without any worry, I wandered along the forest streams and tried to imagine what a tomahawk looked like . . . or, for that matter, a boomerang.

At one in the afternoon I had an appointment with Richard Smiley, head of the environmental department of water control, to discuss water purity standards. We were to meet in a restaurant known as the Index Finger. The restaurant was hidden in an oak grove. From the road a sign in the form of a gigantic finger pointed to it, with the words: "Drop in! You won't be sorry!" The walls of the restaurant were decorated with wild grapes, and by the entrance was a pile of bright orange pumpkins. A shaggy white dog of monstrous size dozed on the porch near the door. I stepped cautiously over it and pushed the door open.

Leaning on the bar was a man with a wine glass in his hand. He was wearing a light gray tailcoat, a white silk scarf, and a sapphire ring on his finger. Silver curls hung loosely to his shoulders, and his long silver brows extended to his temples.

"God, how fancy!" I broke out.

"Thank you, I'm glad you like it," he smiled.

"Please don't think that he is always so good looking," said the woman at the register. "He usually looks pretty ugly. I would even go so far as to say . . . revolting." She took out a pocket mirror and made two careless strokes with her lipstick. I shuddered when I noticed her venom-green face, which was strewn with gold beauty spots.

"Have a seat, please, ma'am. Leila will bring the menu in a moment."

Convinced that I was hallucinating, I rubbed my eyes. Nothing changed. I looked around. The restaurant was otherwise empty except for three middle-aged gentlemen sipping beer in a far corner. I could hear the familiar words "mortgage," "interest," and "taxes." Then the waitress— probably Leila—appeared, wearing a rabbit mask and a lilac bathing suit with a long tail. I squinted.

"Our specialty today is liver with squash and apple pie. Would you like something to drink for starters?"

The telephone rang at the cash register.

"Steven, it's for you," the cashier shouted out to someone inside. The chef, a fat man with a drooping mustache, dressed in a ballet tutu, flew in from the kitchen.

"Hi, kid," he purred into the receiver.

Suddenly from outside the window a shot rang out. That was too much. I screeched and jumped up from my chair.

"There is nothing to worry about," said the gray-haired beauty. "The hunting season has begun. But I can see that you are new to our parts."

I introduced myself and explained why I was there.

"It looks like you were planning to meet me," he said, extending his hand: "Dr. Richard Smiley."

"Very nice to meet you. Do you always dress like this, Dr. Smiley?"

"Unfortunately, no. Only on Halloween."

Oh, Lord! How could I forget! Today is October 31, a day of games, wild costumes, and free treats. The eve of The Day of All Saints.

"I see you celebrate to the fullest, Dr. Smiley."

"Oh, yes! We always take our holidays very seriously and our problems very lightly. Right, Margie?"

"Speak for yourself, Dick," the cashier answered and coquettishly tapped the doctor on the shoulders with a fan. Dr. Smiley looked at his watch.

"Excuse me, I cannot eat with you. I have been stuffing my face with sweets the entire morning and can't even think about lunch. But don't you rush; try everything. Our kitchen is superb. I will go change and will pick you up in forty minutes."

When Dr. Smiley appeared again, his hair was blond and cut short, and he was wearing jeans and a checked shirt. But behind his back hung a marvelous bow and a quiver full of arrows with razor-sharp heads.

"What is that for?" I hesitated, at last reminded of the Simpsons.

"Just in case we run across some deer. In our state shooting deer at this time of the year is allowed only with bows and arrows."

"Dick is no threat," the cashier interjected. "He's been walking around with that bow and arrows for five years now. He hit something only once, and can you guess what it was? A fire engine. Very visible, being that bright red and all."

"Shut up, Margie," the doctor snapped.

When we were seated in his jeep, Dr. Smiley thought for a second.

"You know what? We'll stock up on beer, just in case."

I obediently went back into the Index Finger, bought a dozen Miller-Lights, and offered them to Dr. Smiley.

"Thank you, but I am not particularly fond of beer. It is for you."

"I have no use for it. I don't drink beer."

The doctor said carefully, "It does not hurt to have some beer on you, in case you meet someone in the forest. The Simpsons, for instance . . ."

At that point my supply of optimism had run out. I wanted to be in Brookline, in my own apartment, with the blinds down, the door chained, and the phone unplugged.

I left my car in a parking lot at the Index Finger and got back into Dr. Smiley's Dodge Caravan. We studied the terrain until evening. Then Dr. Smiley drove me back to the restaurant.

"Call if you need anything," he said before driving off. "I am always at your service."

The following morning I woke up at crack of dawn. From the windows of my hotel, the Admiral, I could see blue hills covered with trees as far as the horizon. I felt a chill at the thought that I must now go there. I put a portable measuring device, sterile jars, solutions, etc. — all the usual hydro-geological equipment — into the trunk of my Ford. And on the seat next to me, a wrench . . . Just in case.

While I was driving to the Taosukuits River, the sun came up. I parked the car by the curb and went deep into the woods. The day turned out to be glorious: cool and bright. A small bird with a crimson breast chirped on a tree branch, dry leaves crunched under my feet, and a few rabbits jumped across the paths.

And there was the stream, the border of the Indian reservation, just like on the border of Finland. It was "déjà vu all over again." How long ago was that? Had it happened at all? If so, then it was in my "previous" life. I knelt down, filled a jar with water, and prepared to measure its electrocon-ductivity.

"What the hell are you doing here?"

Startled, I looked up. Above me hovered three Indians, just like living trees. How did they get here? I did not hear any steps, rustling, or crunch-ing of branches. Six narrowed, intent eyes were looking at me. Lord! How I wanted to cover my face with my hands and, squinting, wait until the horrible "eastern" movie ended, the lights came on, and I was able to go home.

"Hi, guys!" I managed to say.

They stood above me, motionless. Leather bands with copper ornaments were pulled tightly across their foreheads, and on their arms were bracelets of the same kind. Two of them had long, black, disheveled hair down to their shoulders; the third had a plaited braid. They were dressed not in hide but in jeans. The sayings on their T-shirts attested to unquestionable cultural progress on the reservation: "Better be active today than radioactive tomorrow," "Split trees, not atoms," and "Best daddy of the year."

"What kind of crap is this?" The brothers looked over my equipment.

Stammering in two great languages, I began to dwell on problems of regional hydrogeology.

"Where are you from?" the fellow with the braid interrupted me.

"From Boston. I work . . ."

"And before Boston where did you live?"

With my heavy Russian accent, could I really disguise the truth? When they heard about the Soviet Union, the men looked at each other.

"That . . . do you know Vasily Alekseev?"

"Lord! Of course! Who doesn't know him! The best weight lifter in the world. Eight times world champion! He is my close friend! We went to high school together!"

Curiosity shone on their previously impenetrable faces. The ice was broken, and suddenly I remembered Dr. Smiley's advice.

"Listen, guys, I have some beer in my trunk. I'm afraid it's warm, but . . ."

"A wonderful idea," they perked up. "We Simpsons never refuse an offer of beer."

We sat in a clearing, opened the beer, and I gave descendants of Wampanoag Indians my first press conference ever. I told them about my former country—about the compulsory military draft in Russia, about the internal passport system, about registration at the local police station, and, more for educational purposes, about the fate of the Crimean Tartars in the former Soviet Union, who were evicted from their native land and forcedly transported to Kazakhstan. The faith of the Crimean Tartars touched them deeply.

"It's just too much," they said, shaking their heads despondently.

The beer was making me drowsy.

"How beautiful it is here, how peaceful."

"Yes, the little place is still quiet," one of the Simpsons asserted. "By the way, we don't live too far away. Just a mile and a half from here, over those hills. So, if you need anything, or something happens, you can count on us."

"What could happen?" I asked absentmindedly.

"All kinds of things. There are some guys over there . . . the Young brothers. You can expect anything from them. Well, it's time for us to go."

They shook my hand and disappeared almost as suddenly as they had appeared. I watched them walk through the golden dry maple leaves covering the ground.

On my way back to my Ford, I looked over my shoulders for any signs of the unpredictable Young brothers.

15 A Broker with a Human Face

Among the Russian emigrants who have lived in the States for five or ten years, we were in the minority who still didn't own any real estate. Let me tell you why. My husband and I were never lucky enough to have jobs simultaneously. Either he was fired or I was laid off. When we surveyed our resources, we realized that if we did buy a house, we would wind up on a steady diet of dog food and Campbell's soup, and that only on national holidays we would be able to afford a visit to McDonald's or Kentucky Fried Chicken.

To tell the truth, we were quite comfortable in our rented apartment, which was quite large and bright. Of course, the ceilings peeled a little, not one window fitted tightly, all our sinks had webs of cracks, and all the faucets dripped. But who in their right mind spends money to fix other people's property? Besides, our apartment was in the heart of a very respectable area. And the rent we paid there was so low that no one would believe it now. God bless rent control!

So what was wrong? Live and be happy! Enjoy the newly found freedoms of expression, press, religion, movement, and assembly. But no. Not owning any real estate undermined our very existence. It is hard to be happy when all your friends are putting steam rooms and saunas in their basements and are building Olympic-size swimming pools. Could one

sleep in peace if those with whom you had worked in a factory for 180 rubles a month a couple of years before were now planting roses in their gar-
dens and owned ponds full of swans and patios with Roman statues? One
cannot sleep in peace. So we didn't.

Every spring we got bitten by the real estate bug. Each Sunday, at seven
in the morning, I would run to Store 24 for the Sunday paper and then
would dash home to spread it out on my floor where, highlighter in hand,
I religiously studied the real estate section. Then I would get on the phone
to call the brokers. We looked at everything from condos and handyman
specials to Tudors and Victorian mansions.

All the brokers in the greater Boston area knew us, hated us, and tried
their best to avoid us. Word got around. Once I came upon an ad: "For
those who have excellent taste, for those who hate to compromise! Marble
fireplaces, mahogany library, billiard room, greenhouse, tennis court—
come to this address, and you will never want to leave it. Finally your
dreams will come true."

That ad was written for me and about me. It is I who have excellent
taste. It is I who hate compromise. So we ran, we saw, and we did not want
to leave. But we did. From time to time we would make an offer, and from
time to time these offers would be accepted. Sometimes, after a sleepless
night, we would call the broker early in the morning and cancel the deal.
Sometimes we got to the structural inspection stage, and then we canceled.
Sometimes we got our deposit back, sometimes we didn't. During all those
years, I figure we lost about $18,000. That's enough for a round-the-world
trip for two or for a studio condo in Iowa.

"The problem is that our taste is not compatible with our means," my
husband Tolya would say.

"You are deeply and tragically wrong," I would answer. "There is a theory that on a fixed income you will never be able to save enough to afford
la dolce vita. You have to get deeply in debt first, then spin like a top, paying a little here and there, and in the meanwhile, live like a king. Remember
the purchase of our Soviet car, Zhiguly?"

The story of the Zhiguly is really educational. One day, in Leningrad, I
passed by the Apraksin Department Store, saw a long line, and, as usual,
asked, "What is it for?" It never hurts to get something really useful for the
household, such as four pounds of oranges or a set of flannel sheets. Or
you might decide to spend a few hours to get something "just in case," like

a subscription for a thirty-four–volume set of the complete oeuvres of Dos-toyevsky. So I asked. It was a line to get a number on the waiting list to buy a car. I didn't have a single ruble in my pocket, I had never had a savings ac-count, and as a Soviet citizen I had never heard of getting a loan from a bank. But I joined the line anyway and stood there for three hours to get a number. I took home the little ticket, and it was my present to Tolya Dargis for his birthday.

Four years passed by. One morning, I found a postcard in my mailbox, inviting us to go to the store and purchase the car. I was so nervous I broke out in a rash and even developed a high fever. What to do? Should we frame the postcard and put it on the wall, or should we actually go ahead and try to grab this fairy-tale bird by its tail? Finally, we started to call all our friends: "Our number came up to buy a car, and we have no money. Could you possibly lend us some dough?"

"What a coincidence," our friends responded. "We also have no money, but our situation is even worse because we are not even on a waiting list."

The next day the phone rang. It was one of my former classmates. After graduation, he had gone to work in the coal mines in the far north to make his fortune. Now, ten years later, he had returned to Leningrad rich, inde-pendent, and ready to party with old friends. "Listen," he said, "what hap-pened to our old gang? Everyone I call begs for money. Nobody even asked what had happened to me during these ten years. Nobody cares how I feel. People treat me as a damn bank. I hope you don't need any dough?"

"God sent you to us. We have a car number, and it has come up."

"Oh well, how much do you need?"

"Fifty-two hundred rubles."

"That's how much the wheel barrow costs?"

"No. It costs fifty-five hundred."

"How come you have three hundred?"

As you see, we were known for not having any money. He brought us the cash in two briefcases. Soviet citizens don't have credit cards or check-books. We took the briefcases, got on a bus, and went to buy our car. All the way to the Apraksin Dvor department store we dreamt about our fu-ture. Next summer, we would drive across the Baltic republics—Estonia, Latvia, and Lithuania—or we might even drive down to the shores of the Black Sea to visit our friends in Odessa, which, like New York, never sleeps.

We were brought back to reality by the bus driver, who called out the name of our stop, and we ran for the door. Only after we had caught our breath on the sidewalk did I ask my husband, "Well, Tolya, where are the briefcases?" and he answered, "I thought you had them."

How he raced down the street after the bus, how the pedestrians scattered and ran for cover, how the police sirens followed, and how the ambulance skidded—all of this is the subject of another story. Suffice it to say that we retrieved our money, bought our treasured Zhiguly automobile, and visited all our dream spots. Moreover, we paid off our northern Santa Claus within three years. The question is: How come that in the ten years after graduation, with both of us working, my husband and I were not able to save enough to buy one tire?

During all these years of house hunting, I became a renowned expert on real estate in Boston and vicinity. The houses listed in my memory already had changed hands three times and had tripled in value. I knew all the street names and house numbers by heart. I was well acquainted with every house style, as well as with years of construction and first and last owners. I became an authority on percolation tests, plumbing problems, sewer systems, electrical amperage, roof qualities, down spouts, flashing, and the daytime and nocturnal habits of carpenter ants, powder post beetles, termites, squirrels, and raccoons. I was on a first-name basis with bankers, home inspectors, lawyers, and engineers. Yet I owned no property.

One beautiful Sunday morning I awoke particularly depressed. A hopelessly dull day lay ahead of me. After having a psychoanalytic session with myself, I realized that the cause of my depression was, as usual, "still a tenant, not an owner."

"Shall I do something wild and crazy?" my alter ego asked my ego. "What kind of craziness do you have in mind?" my ego replied.

"Finally buy a condo this very day," suggested my alter ego.

"With what money?"

"Don't we have Russian friends anymore?" asked my alter ego. "And what happened to all our American friends, all those bankers and mortgage officers?"

As Russian emigrants say in their Pidgin English, "Not you worry."

I went out onto the street. The autumn day was clear and serene. Yellow and scarlet leaves rustled at my feet. The air was still and fresh.

"This is exactly what we will do," both egos agreed. "We will pop into the first agency we see, we will ask to be shown a condo, and we will buy it this very day!"

The first real estate agency I spotted on the avenue, just one block from my apartment, was a newly opened office. With luck, its brokers didn't know me. Feeling suicidal, I pushed open the glass door. At a table sat a middle-aged woman in a black cowboy hat, a pink, ruffled man's shirt, and black tuxedo trousers. In the corner of her mouth she balanced a cigarette while at the same time chewing pumpkin seeds and talking to someone on the phone. Without looking at me she pointed to a chair and also to a sign on her desk, "Brenda Morgan, Realtor Extraordinaire."

I sat and tried to understand her side of the phone conversation. She obviously was attacking someone. But all of a sudden, she burst out in a contagious laugh and hung up the receiver.

"In this business, you have to be a bull. Otherwise, they crush you. Can I help you?"

"I'd like to buy a condo."

"How many have you seen?"

"Well, enough."

"How long have you been looking?"

"About two years."

Brenda yawned and lit another cigarette.

"Where do you live now?"

"Just around the corner. We rent a three-bedroom apartment, two baths, a dining room, and a living room with a fireplace. It's really a wonderful flat, but it's in terrible condition. Nobody has done any repairs for a hundred years, and our landlord is going to double our rent."

"Bastard . . . But what do you want? Describe to me the condo of your dreams."

"Three bedrooms, two baths, a dining room, and a living room with a fireplace. And I would like to stay in this area, of course."

"In other words, you want your apartment, but you want to own it."

"Oh—huh."

"You're lucky. I have twenty minutes before my next appointment, so I'll show you one property."

Brenda took a key from her drawer, tilted her hat on her forehead, and walked to the door. "Are we going in your car?" I asked.

"No car. We walk."

We turned the corner onto my Morton Street.

"Look, Brenda, we live in that building on the third floor."

Bored, Brenda nodded, crossed the street, and stopped in front of exactly the same kind of building, with exactly the same kind of courtyard. It was a mirror image of our building.

"It would be funny if this condo was on the third floor."

"Why?"

"Because we live on the third floor, in apartment number six."

When we reached the third floor, Brenda took out her key and opened the door of apartment number six. There were indeed three bedrooms, two bathrooms, a dining room, and a living room with a fireplace. Everything I had dreamed of.

"Brenda, how much does it cost?"

"Two hundred and twenty-five thousand dollars."

"Oh. Then it's not for us. Too expensive."

"How much can you afford?"

"A hundred and fifty tops."

"Well, the situation looks pretty lousy." Brenda pushed her hat brim up. "So what in the hell are we doing here? We have to look for something smaller."

"I don't want anything smaller," said I with tears running down my cheeks.

From the living room windows I could see the golden leaves of the old maple tree and could look into my rented apartment across the courtyard.

"Well, well," said Brenda, pacing as she lit another cigarette. "On the one hand, a hundred fifty thousand is laughable. On the other, it's nothing to sneeze at either. The owners of this condo have already moved to Florida, and keeping their condo on the market doesn't make them any happier. Maybe it's worth a shot."

We returned to her office. Brenda picked up the phone and dialed the Florida number. "Mrs. Berman. Good morning. Brenda here. I have wonderful news for you." I heard a cheerful chirp through the receiver but no words. "Very solid clients," Brenda said in a deep contralto voice, "and your condo suits them more or less. Of course it needs tremendous renovation. They figure they'll have to spend no less than fifty thousand to bring it up to their standards."

I thought about the condo. Where possibly could I invest fifty thousand dollars? Maybe to install a marble bathtub, or a crystal sink, or a platinum refrigerator. It sounded like Mrs. Berman asked how much these solid clients were offering.

"Well, I don't know yet. They saw a few other places that pleased them as well as yours. It's fall, you see, and the market here is very slow. I'll call you in a couple of days." Brenda hung up. "Okay now—your husband has to see this place tonight, and if he loves it as much as you do, we will try to cut a deal."

That very same evening, my husband saw it, and it was love at first sight.

"Brenda, please, call Mrs. Berman and tell her what we are offering."

"Out of the question. We will wait."

The next morning, I ran to the agency with a written offer of hundred fifty thousand dollars. I hadn't slept all night out of fear that this condo would slip away from under my nose. Brenda hardly looked at my offer and shoved it in the drawer.

"Why don't you call it in?"

"Because you want it too much, and I am giving . . ."

At that moment, the phone rang. It was Miami.

"Mrs. Berman. What a nice surprise. How is sunny Florida? How is your husband? What about your mother? How's the weather affecting her rheumatism? . . . My clients? Oh, I am seeing them this afternoon and showing them three more condos. It's hard to say. The condo market is really flooded. There must be more than two hundred units on the market right now. I'll see what I can do . . . But if they do make an offer, I'm afraid it'll be in the mid hundreds."

"Oh, no!" Miami screamed, and the conversation ended.

"Go home," Brenda said to me. "Take your husband out to lunch. Go to a movie or browse around a museum. There is an African art exhibition that's worth seeing. Don't think about the damn condo. When I have any news, I'll find you."

Obviously, Mrs. Berman's nerves were rattled. She called Brenda back within an hour. Brenda told her that these clients were Jewish immigrants from the Soviet Union. They were refuseniks and had waited for a visa to the States for five years. Back in Mother Russia, they were well-known professors and members of the Academy of Science. But here in America, they had to clean apartments while they were learning the language and local customs. They had to walk to their work because they had no car and saved every penny they could. And finally they had saved ten thousand dollars for a down payment on a condo.

Brenda was so shaken by her own speech, that her voice cracked and two tears ran down her cheeks. Mrs. Berman also had a little cry because her grandparents were from Russia, and, although they had not been members of the Academy of Science over there, they had also started by washing floors. In later years Mrs. Berman's father managed to buy a few drugstores, so Mrs. Berman herself did not grow up in poverty. Also, her marriage was quite satisfactory—Mr. Berman owned a packaging factory.

"Generally speaking, the Bermans don't really need this money," said Brenda. "They just hate the idea of not getting a fair market price."

"Listen Brenda, why are you trying so hard to help us? The more you sell for, the more you make. Isn't that so?"

"Yes, it is so. But you see I'm not an ordinary broker." She pointed to the sign on her desk: Realtor Extraordinaire. "I have my own pride and my own philosophy."

Brenda took off her hat and threw it on the floor. Her short, curly hair looked like a head of cauliflower. "All mankind can be divided into two uneven groups: the larger group suffers from lack of money, the smaller has plenty but doesn't know what to do with it. I am somewhere in between. The way I see it, you cannot make all the money in the world, and even if you can, what the hell for?"

For a middle-aged American woman, that was not a trivial declaration— at least it went against what we had been taught in Russia about Americans.

"How long have you been in this business?" I asked.

"About a decade. Before that I taught Hebrew. I have a masters' degree in Judaic studies."

"Why did you go into real estate?" I pressed on, intrigued.

"Because when I left my husband my salary wasn't enough to support my daughter and myself. By the way, my ex-husband is very charming, a kind and gentle man. I think you would like him."

"Why did you . . . ?"

"He was so boring! He gave me a nineteen-year-long headache. Well, I think it's about time to call Florida. Here we go!"

She dialed. "Hello, Mrs. Berman. What a hell of a day I've had. I managed to pull out another five thousand from the Russians. They are now at one forty-five. If I were you, I'd grab it and run. What? One fifty? I'm afraid we'll lose them. I don't believe you want this condo to be on the market in the dead of winter. The snow gets pretty deep in Boston, you know. You're really pushing, dear, but I'll give it another shot. Bye."

"Brenda, I can't believe my ears. Did we buy it?"

"Looks like it. Call your husband. Get him here, and we'll wrap it up."

The structural inspection, running from bank to bank, applications, appraisals, purchase and sale agreement, and mortgage commitment took about two months. The day of the closing finally arrived. Tolya and I were delirious—it was the first time we would have owned our very own place. We ordered a truck, and when the move was over, the owner of the moving company sent us his bill: three hours of packing and carrying it down from the third floor, two minutes of transportation, and four hours of bringing the stuff up to the third floor. Altogether, eight hundred dollars. We were too happy to be furious.

When I next saw Brenda in her office, I began to weep.

"What is it?" grumbled Brenda, "Take a Valium."

"What if we can't pay the mortgage? What if my husband is laid off? What if he gets sick and disabled?"

"Jesus Christ," said Brenda in a Woody Allen voice. "I studied Dostoyevsky in high school. We were taught that the Russians just love to suffer, but not to this extent. I think you are nuts. Try to be happy for a minute. Shut off the waterworks, will you? And go find a solid job, for God's sake."

"Who needs me? Who needs an expert in clay and sand in Boston? If I lose my present job nobody will hire me again."

"What are you talking about? What does sand and clay have to do with anything? Go into the real world. Go into the real estate business. Even without a license, you already know a lot."

"Me? Sell houses? I could never. Not in this lifetime."

"Bullshit! Go to the Realty Institute, take the course, pass the exam, and start making money. By the way, the Institute is located just around the corner."

"Thank you, Brenda, thank you for everything, for all your help and advice. I will think about it. Maybe in the spring, like in April."

"Not in April—on Monday!" roared Brenda as she hit her desk with her fist. "This Monday at nine A.M. And I never want to hear any more of your whining. This is America, the land of great real estate and great opportunities. Go sign up and make it happen. It's not going to come to you; you have to go after it."

From anger, her eyes had become round, her cheeks had puffed out, and if she only had a thin mustache above her lip, she would have been a carbon copy of the famous Russian tzar, Peter the Great.

"Okay, okay," I mumbled, backing off to the door. "On Monday I will enroll. Thank you again. Good-bye."

And I retreated from the agency. In the corridor, I took a deep breath, powdered my nose, and knocked on the door again. Brenda was in a lively discussion with somebody on the phone. When she saw me return, she put the other person on hold.

"Something new happening? A new tragedy?"

"No, no. I just want to ask you—suppose I do take the course, and suppose by some miracle I pass the exam, who will hire me? No experience, no connections, and quite poor English."

"Me! Me, you damn fool! I will hire you!" Brenda bellowed, "In this office at that desk."

"But why? Why would you? Why do you need me?"

"Because you will be my bridge to Boston's Russian clients. Listen to me, tragic Pavlova, you are going to work for me, and I will make a real broker out of you, tough, resourceful, and aggressive."

"But Brenda, were you yourself tough and aggressive in closing our deal?"

"Of course I was. You don't even know the whole story. I not only tried hard for you, but I charged only half of the commission. Not typical, you say? Well, the more you know me, the more you will learn that I do business my way. I wanted to do you a favor. However, I also did a favor to the Bermans. Their apartment was sitting on the market for four months and was bound to sit there until spring. And they did make a nice profit on it. Less than they wanted, but they more than doubled their investment. So nobody got hurt and everybody is happy."

Brenda came from behind her desk and gave me a big hug. "Let me know what you want for a house warming present."

16 Born Again at Howard Johnson's

Yes, it happened exactly the way I was afraid it would. Four month after we bought our condo my company lost a big contract and the entire geology department was closed. However, during this time, thanks to Brenda's persistence, I managed to take a real estate course and even passed both exams. Brenda kept her word and, as promised, took me into her office. I got a desk, a phone, a computer, and even a brass name plate that said, *"Tatyana Dargis—Capitalistic Barracuda."*

The real estate business was lousy that season. I could not make a single sale or list a single property. Brenda greeted me every morning with, "Well? What do you have to say for yourself? Again nothing?"

I tried to follow each sale-by-owner ad in the newspaper, but every time I found a lead, I was met with the same line, "We have already listed our property with Millie Monroe."

"Again Millie Monroe?" Brenda chided. "If I hear that name once more I'll scream! Go undercover and find out her secret, or else . . ."

With my job in jeopardy, I moved on my assignment. Spying was a new role for me. Back in the former Soviet Union, it was I who was spied upon. But as life goes on, roles sometimes reverse. I came up with a three-step plan. First, I studied Millie Monroe's most recent ad:

> Isn't it time to stop making your landlord rich? Isn't it time to build your own nest? Isn't it time to look down upon your neighbors from your own French Normandy?

> **Half acre rolling land with English garden. Gracious living-room with marble fireplace, four lush bedrooms; three Spanish tile bathrooms with bidet for discriminating buyer; library; garage convertible to mother-in-law suite: you will never know she is there.**
>
> **A steal at $1,200,000.**

Such an ad costs a fortune. Brenda, with her keen sense of economy, would have promoted that very same property this way: "French Normandy, 4 BD, 3 BA, firepl., libr., gar., 1/2 acre, $1,200,000."

To learn Millie's technique for getting listings, I placed a phony ad in the paper pretending I wanted to sell my house. Actually, I did not own a house, but that was a minor detail. Sure enough, the very first phone call was from Millie—she had taken the bait.

"Hello. This is Millie Monroe from Regal Realty. I noticed your very well-written ad in this morning's paper. It just so happens that I have a psychiatrist coming in from Vienna this very day. He must buy a home this weekend, and he is an all-cash buyer. May I please bring him to your home in fifteen minutes?"

"No brokers, please. I intend to sell my house myself."

"What a pity! I can get you a very good price."

"But your commission . . ."

"Don't worry about that. I will bring you an offer you cannot refuse. Can we just stop by and have a peek?"

"No, I am leaving for the weekend. Sorry." And I hung up.

The phone rang again. "Hello, it's Millie again. I believe we were disconnected. When will you return?"

"Not earlier than Monday night."

"By what time?"

"Well, I don't know . . . Around ten o'clock, I suppose."

"Wonderful, then we will be at your place at 10:15. I do hope my client loves your house, and if so, we can complete the deal in two weeks. What is your address, please?"

Charm trickled like warm molasses through the receiver into my ear and down to my heart. I was ready to sell my imaginary house to her imaginary

Dr. Freud, sight unseen. But I pulled myself together and said to her what other homeowners had said to me so many times: "Thanks, but I am going to try to sell it myself."

"May I call you in a week to find how things are going? If you still don't sell, I will be happy to help. And I'd like to meet with you during the week and just take a look at your beautiful house. How about in an hour? I will take only ten minutes of your time." I couldn't stand it anymore and simply hung up on her.

Back in my office, I reported to Brenda. Not saying a word to me, she picked up the phone. "Hello Millie? This is Brenda from B & B Realty. I have something that I would like to discuss with you. Can you come to my office tomorrow at noon? Super. I will see you then."

Millie Monroe showed up in our agency promptly at noon. She was dressed to kill. Millie was over fifty, with a neat, short haircut and bright wide-open gray eyes full of the world's joy. Her skin was silky, and her teeth sparkled. A symphony of middle-aged grace.

Brenda didn't mince words: "Millie, what is the secret of your success? We've known each other for at least a decade, and your agency and mine were about equal in sales during all this time. This season you've cornered the market. What is it? As I recall, I sent a few good deals your way last year when I went on vacation. Come on, level with me."

Millie put a hand to her lips and giggled.

"Yes, Brenda dear, I remember. And yes, you're looking at the new Millie, and there's a good reason for it. I've been 'born again.'"

"What are you talking about?"

"You mean you haven't heard about it?"

"About what?" Brenda was getting quite annoyed.

"About 'Realization.' You won't believe it, girls, but after this experience I am a totally new person. I was born again. A miracle, simply a miracle."

"What in hell are you rambling about, Millie?" Brenda asked impatiently.

"It's hard to describe. I threw away all my antidepressants. I got in touch with my feelings. I have risen above all pettiness. I am loved by everybody, and I myself love people again. I even tolerate my brother, whom I haven't spoken to for six years. He has always been such a jerk."

"What happened? Did he suddenly get rich or smart or what?"

"No, he hasn't changed. It's me. I've even taken on a young lover who serves me coffee in bed every morning."

"Too bad you were not born again three husbands ago," Brenda snapped.

"Come on, Brenda. You asked, now hear me out. Take, for instance, my sister-in-law, whom I barred from my threshold four Christmases ago when she sent me some cheap slippers from Woolworth's. She is now one of my best friends. The world is lovely, the sun is shining, and it's just so great to be alive."

"You're showing early signs of senility," quipped Brenda, not really knowing how to react to this gush of optimism. "But what about real estate?"

"Business is great since I finally got rid of my shyness. It's impossible to intimidate me anymore. Nothing is easier for me now than to knock on doors and talk the owners into listing their houses with me. To tell you the truth, this year I made more money than I did in the five previous years combined."

"Now you're talking my language." Brenda was always turned on by money. "Okay, what in hell is your 'Realization'?"

"Well, it's a process of self-awakening through playing certain games and meditation. You have to experience it yourself. I'm afraid I'll spoil it for you if I give away more details now."

"And what is the price for such a miraculous and mysterious awakening?"

"Only five hundred bucks. And, girls, I highly recommend it to you."

"What's in it for you?" my straightforward boss asked.

"If I recruit you and you sign up, I get to participate in the graduate seminar held in the Himalayas for half price."

"Himalayas? To whom are you going to sell real estate there? Wise men of the mountains live in caves or monasteries. Or are you counting on Bigfoot?"

While Brenda and Millie were bantering, I was thinking about the five hundred dollars. For that kind of money I could buy a ticket to Paris, spend a weekend in Barbados, buy forty quarts of generic Vodka, get a new kitchen table and four chairs, get a year's membership in the health club . . . I never had money for any of those things. Besides, I didn't need to improve family relations. I didn't have any brothers or sisters. Tolya Dargis was still an angel after twenty years of happy marriage. My daughter and son-in-law lived in California, and though they also send me cheap slippers from Woolworth's every Christmas, I didn't feel bad about it. I promptly sent these slippers to my girlfriends as Hanukkah or birthday presents.

"Do you want to enroll?" asked Brenda.

"No, I don't want to enroll," I said firmly.

"Why not?" Brenda's bifocals suddenly sparkled. "If we're going to make a ton of money from it, we should give it a shot. But you had better be right, Millie old girl, or else I will find a way to get even with you. Okay, where do we sign up?"

So, one Thursday evening, Brenda and I showed up at the local Howard Johnson's. I hadn't slept much the night before, mainly because I had no idea of what to expect. No such psychological workshops existed in Russia, my native country. Psychiatrists, psychologists, and all other "psy's" were dangerous people there. You would not want to have their names on your official record, nor would you want your name on their official records. Your record followed you forever, and in my time, if you didn't behave like a flock of sheep, you could well find yourself in a very cold cuckoo nest. Finally, I calmed down and decided that my emotional stance would be that of an observer, a spectator, rather than that of a participant.

In the luxurious main ballroom of our Howard Johnson's the mirrors shone, the crystal chandeliers sparkled, and one hundred and forty participants settled down in crimson velvet chairs. A puny-looking fellow appeared on the stage. His three-piece suit was stylish, his movements fluid and graceful. He took the microphone and brought it very close to his mouth, stroking it like a delicate brandy goblet.

"Hello, dear friends. I am Giovanni Denino, your leader. My parents immigrated from Italy, and I was born in California. I did my graduate work at UCLA, but I spent most of my life selling pizza and soaking in a Jacuzzi."

"Great combination, psychiatry and pizza," Brenda muttered under her breath. "During therapy, I can order an antipasto."

Ten minutes earlier she had written a check for a thousand dollars for both of us to this pizza man. Brenda hated to part with money and was in a very bad mood. "Can you imagine," she whispered leaning toward me, "a hundred and forty times $500 equals $70,000. That's how much HE 'realized' this weekend."

"Sh-sh . . ."

"One day, soaking amid the bubbles and feeling particularly lonely," continued our leader, "I touched toes with a woman who was touching toes with another man. Unfortunately for me, he turned out to be her husband, but we began to chat, and they invited me to a free seminar that they were leading entitled 'Rediscover Yourself.' I went, and here I am today, bringing the good news to you. Together, we will be looking into issues like 'you and yourself.' Are you, for instance, acquainted with your soul? Are you in touch with your body and your feelings? How do you know that you are really alive? I will speak on these and many other crucial issues. Tonight we start our workshop. We will be working for four days, a total of about fifty-two hours. In this room, only I will have the right to wear a watch. Please, everybody, take off your watches. Note taking and tape recorders are also strictly forbidden."

We fumbled around our wrists, grumbling.

He continued: "This weekend, you should not take any medications. Forget about sleeping pills, caffeine, Valium, Alka-Seltzer, aspirins, uppers or downers. You take nothing at all."

"What about my asthma?" Brenda shouted out.

"I repeat. No medicine. This weekend, you will have no time to be sick, believe me. Look around you. What do you see? Unfamiliar, cold faces. I am sure that many of you look at each other with fear and suspicion. Monday, I promise, you will love each other dearly. I assume that in the psychological baggage that you have brought with you we can find such garbage as low self-esteem, unfulfillment, general tiredness, and loneliness . . . Wait till Monday. You will feel younger, energetic, full of newly found strength and lust for life. But these days will not be easy for you. It will be a dramatic emotional experience. You will go through purgatory and through hell, and in fifty-two hours you will be born all over again. You will rise from the ashes like the proverbial bird Phoenix."

"Good Lord! I would pay anything for that," someone whispered behind my back.

"They certainly didn't charge you enough," Brenda snapped.

Giovanni overheard her remark and raised his voice. "So, you will be reborn, and your new identity will conquer your old one. You will find your true self, you will come back to your real self and love it."

He stopped and bowed gracefully, waiting for applause. But the audience was frozen in anticipation of the promised transformation. Behind the wall, in the restaurant kitchen, 'untransformed' waitresses made a rattle with forks and knives. From the fifth row, a man rose and started to walk to the exit.

"Excuse me, sir. Just a minute. Where are you going?"

"To the rest room."

"Come back and be seated," Giovanni ordered. "You have to control your biological needs. You are allowed to go to the rest rooms, to eat, smoke, and drink, but only during official breaks. They will occur every four hours."

"But I cannot be born again on a full bladder."

Some meek giggles spread through the audience. Some brave participants even applauded. Giovanni scowled and made a forceful gesture demanding silence.

"No self-indulgence. No physiological interference. Our work requires absolute concentration. You will see for yourself that one can cope. So, please sit down, mister . . ."

"My name is Charles Green. I insist, if you don't mind." With these words he walked out.

"Alright, ladies and gentlemen, let us begin our first exercise. Under your chairs you will find an envelope. Please open it now and look at the labels. Each of the eight labels has a word printed on it: *'aloof,' 'sly,' 'attractive,' 'ugly,' 'sincere,' 'friendly,' 'scary,' 'distrustful.'* When you hear the bell, take a walk around the room looking at faces and attach all your labels to various people. Choose a person and label him. You are allowed to explain to them why you are giving them this label by using only one sentence that begins with, 'I give you this label because . . .' Only one sentence. When you receive a label, do not converse or argue. Simply say 'Thank you.' You will repeat this procedure eight times until you use up all the labels. After that, you will display labels that you received on your chest and gather in small groups of nine or ten people each. Then you will have a chance to tell your group what you feel about how others judged you and whether this is the way you see yourself. Good luck!"

A bell sounded. We wandered around the ballroom and stared intently at one another. Some people smiled openheartedly. Others, with tense faces, squeezed themselves into the corners of the hall, afraid to look around and trying to become invisible. I was one of these. Drops of cold sweat were running down my back, my knees were trembling, and I had a splitting headache. I could not get hold of myself and had no idea why I was so upset. Silently I begged everyone, "Don't look at me, don't stamp me, don't brand me." They seemed to be able to read my mind, and I received only three labels: "attractive," "aloof," and "sly."

Attractive—oh, yes, I couldn't agree more. But aloof and sly? "I'm scared to death!" I wanted to shout, but instead, I bowed and mumbled "Thank you."

It was very easy to give a stranger a "nice" label, like "friendly" or "attractive," and even not-so-nice "aloof." But what about "scary" or "distrustful"? I did the best I could—I threw those into the wastebasket. Still, I kept three in my pocket: "sly," "ugly," and "sincere." I approached a very pretty girl, gave her "ugly," and said, "I give you this label because you know how beautiful you are, and I'm sure you won't be offended."

The label "sincere" I gave to Charlie Green. Charlie's chest, looking like an admiral's, was already adorned with several positive labels.

The label "sly" I pinned on a man who looked like a Harvard professor, saying, "I give you this because it's my last one." He smiled.

Brenda had managed to accumulate sixteen labels: one "attractive," three "sincere," five "ugly," and seven "distrustful." She muttered, "Crazy bastards! How can I be sincere and distrustful at the same time? What a bunch of lunatics. Let's get out of here!"

"Brenda, it's only a game."

"Yeah, but who am I? Tell me who I am."

"Wait till Monday. You'll find out."

In my mini-group sat a young man, Doug, who had a punk haircut and one gigantic silver earring. He received seventeen negative labels, among them several each of "aloof" and "scary." He was on the verge of tears, absolutely crushed and miserable. "Am I scary? Why don't people trust me?" he confided during the break.

Doug's family was not typical middle-American. His father was a gay artist who lived abroad. His mother, a Lesbian actress, lived in Hollywood. Doug was raised by his grandmother, who was deeply hurt and embarrassed by her daughter and son-in-law. And she managed to convey these feelings to Doug quite successfully. Shy and lonely, he responded with a grateful smile to my smallest kind gesture. His "Phoenix" had a difficult journey ahead.

The next exercise was meditation. "Sit down in your chairs and relax," our leader instructed. "Drop your shoulders, stretch out your legs, let your lower jaw hang loosely. When the lights dim, close your eyes and listen to the music. Think back to a time when you felt extremely hurt, when you had been an innocent victim. In fifteen minutes a bell will sound, and then the people in every odd-numbered row will turn 180 degrees and face the people in the even row, knee to knee. All persons facing the rear of the room will have one minute to tell their story to their vis-à-vis. The listener must not say a word. Then you will switch roles."

The ballroom was drowned in darkness. Funeral chapel music was playing softly. A violin complained, a cello responded bitterly, while a piano wept along. I recognized Tchaikovsky's Trio, which I had studied for five years. With my defiant nature I cannot relax or be sad on demand. I tried hard, but I could not conjure up even one tiny hurt, moral or physical. I started to giggle, and then all my efforts were directed at controlling myself.

So, there I sat among a hundred and forty obedient people with hanging jaws who had paid good money to sit in Howard Johnson's on the Charles River. Outside, the sun was shining, Filene's Basement was full of bargains, and in the Chinese restaurant next door the sweet and sour soup was waiting.

All of a sudden in the far corner of the room somebody burst into a mournful wail. Then another one sobbed loudly. At my right, a young fellow was weeping with his head between his knees. Ten minutes later the whole ballroom was awash with tears. It sounded like a kennel before feeding time. The urge to cry was contagious. My nose tickled, a lump swelled in my throat, and my eyes filled up with tears.

The bell rang. A pretty young woman turned her chair around and faced me. She stretched out her hands to me. Black mascara streamed down her cheeks. "My husband and I have been happily married for five years." She started sobbing. "We both worked hard, bought a house, and joined a time-sharing resort in Mexico. We decided not to have any children. Why should we kill ourselves? Why should we spend all our savings on their education? My husband agreed: 'Let's live for ourselves.' But my parents nagged for grandchildren. They promised to baby-sit and give us clothing and toys and everything. So I had a little girl. And you know what happened? They moved to Connecticut. And for two years we had to hire a baby-sitter. I still don't talk to my parents . . . You should see my daughter. She is absolutely beautiful. She is so cheerful and happy and brings me great joy."

This exercise was designed to teach us how to spill our guts and, more importantly, how to listen. But I broke the rule of silence and interrupted. "Wait a minute dear. I must've missed something. I don't understand why you are crying."

"Because . . . they promised . . . my parents . . . and I believed them. They tricked me and moved away, and I hate them. So what if my father got a good job there? He should've found one here."

I was shocked. What a spoiled, rotten brat this young woman turned out to be. "Wait a minute," I thought. "Now I will tell you *my* story and will really make you weep."

"Once I had a fiancé. He was more gorgeous than Paul Newman, and I was crazy about him. God, how I loved him! We were the happiest couple on earth and were going to get married after his service in the army. You know, in Russia every boy over eighteen must serve in the armed forces . . . So he was drafted into the army for three years.

"I never dated anyone all that time. I never went to a bar or to a movie. I wrote to him every single day. And every single weekend I spent with his deaf-and-dumb grandmother . . . Finally he returned and we got married. I was working three jobs so he could study at the university. I cooked, I cleaned, I did his laundry and his homework. I even invited his deaf-and-dumb grandmother to stay with us.

"Then I got pregnant. A few days before I was due, he disappeared. I found a note under my pillow saying that the magic was gone and he didn't love me any more. He simply ran away together with my TV, my food processor, my cross-country skis, my cactus plant, and Jim the cat. He left me his grandmother, though. I was calm until I found out about Jim. That was too much. I was in such a state of shock that I went into labor right then and there. I delivered the creature all by myself. It didn't look like a girl, and I could not tell for certain it was a boy . . . It looked more like Jim the cat . . ."

At that moment I regretted getting so carried away with my joke. The girl fainted and fell to the floor. Someone came to her rescue, and I was delighted that a break was announced. People dried their tears and rushed to the rest rooms and the cafeterias.

The second half of the first evening was ushered in with loud trumpets as the theme for the movie *Rocky* blasted through the public announcement system. This was to become our anthem, and we quickly learned to react to it like Pavlov's dogs by taking the last drags on our cigarettes, gulping down the rest of our coffee, and rushing to our seats like obedient little girls and boys. During this session, we were given a two-hour lecture about the loneliness of individuals in a high-tech society.

"People are afraid of each other. People distrust each other. They keep forgetting that every one of us has secret complexes: self-hatred, fear of old age, of poverty, of illness and death. People are weak and imperfect. You must learn to love yourself the way you are and yet try to improve yourself. Now, we are going to play a few games. Soon you will discover their deep and lasting significance. You will learn that you are not alone in the world. There is great comfort in knowing that we are really all the same. There are countless groups that we can fit into and associate ourselves with. There are so many common denominators that bind us . . . For instance, the color of our underwear! So, we are about to start our first game. Please focus on the color of your underpants, then find others with the same color, and form groups. I'll give you a few seconds to look at your own in case you don't remember."

We jumped up and shouted out loud our colors—pink! red! white! blue! green! Groups formed. I was surprised to learn that some folks had come to the seminar without any underwear at all. They formed the largest and the most powerful group called "none."

The second game was aimed at grouping people with the same naughty personal habits. We were asked to shout out our most embarrassing secrets. We were getting into the spirit, and the room resounded with "Peeing in the shower!" "Nose picking!" "Nail biting!" "Shoplifting!" "Masturbation!" "Eavesdropping!" What a great time we were having. We were shouting out the words we never dared to think aloud. This was totally liberating. I was free at last!

But the third game was very scary for me. Giovanni asked us to choose the animal we would like to be in our next life. There were only three options—a pig, a chicken, or a cow. The animals were supposed to be blind, Giovanni told us. We had to crawl on the floor trying to find our siblings by making the sound of the animal of our choice. On our hands and knees, with closed eyes, we oinked, clucked, and mooed our way across the floor. A huge crowd of cluckers assembled and hugged each other. We bumped heads, and one lady chicken, for no apparent reason, bit the ear of an oinker who turned out to be a lawyer. The oinker stood up, stopped oinking, and ran to Giovanni, threatening to sue him for damages. They were screaming at one another in the middle of this swarming and crawling animal farm. I hid in the corner, looked at the crowd, and recalled the funeral of Joseph Stalin.

I was just a youngster, but I clearly remembered the horror of those days. Millions of Soviet people lived under his regime like naive, stupid cows, submissive pigs, and cowardly chickens, blinded by fear or admiration. When he died, they all converged on the Kremlin to pay their last respects. During the stampede thousands were trampled and killed. Overcome by this wave of reminiscence, I entered a tunnel of deep depression and could not enjoy the rest of the evening.

More instructions followed: "Please choose a partner. One person will be a piece of clay, the other the sculptor. The chunks of clay must sink to their hands and knees, with their heads hanging loosely downward. The sculptors are free to do with the clay anything they wish."

The sculptors extended and bent the limbs of the clay and created their masterpieces in three minutes. Some clays screamed in pain, but who cared? We learned to be submissive. Then the Pygmalions walked around the room, admiring their creations and choosing the most beautiful ones. Then the roles were reversed. My sculptor was a boring young woman with no imagination. She made me cross my legs and my arms, and I became a pretzel. But Brenda's sculptor turned out to be a creative sadist. Brenda hurt everywhere, and she limped for days after. "How in hell can I make money in this condition?" she groaned.

The next day the atmosphere was lighter and friendlier. The *Rocky* trumpets sounded, and the workshop started with a new meditation. Our leader asked us to concentrate on our relationship with our parents.

"I'm sure many of you carry guilt feelings toward your parents. Would you like to get rid of them? Imagine that you have just entered the room where your mother is sitting in a comfortable chair. Hug her, kiss her, and tell her what is in your heart. Nobody on earth can understand you better. See her smile. You are being heard. You are forgiven. Cry if you feel like it, and at long last be free."

The light has dimmed, and mournful music filled the room. People started to cry again. Brenda pressed her forehead against the chair in front of her and wept. I knew that her mother had died seven years before. I also knew that they had loved each other deeply and had been the closest friends. Her old father was an arrogant and difficult man, and Brenda still feared him and tried desperately to please him. Why was she weeping so hard, my cold calculating boss? And what was my own heart made of?

I suddenly recalled something that happened when I was fifteen years old. I had brought home a very special boy. We had planned to go ice-skating and I needed heavy socks. I looked for them in all my drawers but in vain. My mother was home, and I asked her where they were. She went to a closet and pulled out a pair with huge holes. She held them up high above my head, then turned to the boy and asked, "Did you know that your girlfriend is such a slob?" And then she slapped my face with the socks. I could never talk to that boy again, and now, as I tried very hard to imagine my mother in a chair, I saw her holding up those awful socks with huge holes in them. When the lights finally brightened, many hands rose in the air—people were eager to share their feelings.

The first to take the stage was a seventeen-year-old girl. She was a high school student, with heavy make-up, braces on her teeth, and dressed very expensively.

"You cannot imagine how upset I am," she wept. "I never shared my problems with any living person, but now I am compelled to tell it all to you."

I was prepared to hear a horrifying drama about child abuse, for instance, that her father raped her, her mother committed suicide, or her brother killed her father with a kitchen knife.

"I attend a very fancy boarding school, and I visit my parents on the weekends. Would you believe that my parents won't give me the keys to the car so I can go to the beach? My father still calls me 'baby' and 'sweetheart.' When my parents go out, my brother bites me and pinches me. He was really mad when I mailed two letters to my friends with some expensive old stamps from his collection. How was I supposed to know? I hate them all. Last week, I hid myself in the basement closet. My parents searched for me for three hours and even called the police. Why did I do it? To get back at them. My mother is a real idiot. She didn't let me go to Honolulu on spring break with my best friend's family. You know what she said? 'First learn how to make money yourself.' What a bitch! She never ever worked herself. If you people only knew how much money my father makes. He could wallpaper the whole house with hundred-dollar bills." She wept in her hands.

Our instructor Giovanni Denino approached her and embraced her tenderly. "Imagine please that you have just entered the room where your mother is sitting in a comfortable chair. Hug her, kiss her, and tell her all your troubles. Nobody on earth can understand you better."

The next speaker, another high school student, also bitterly complained about his parents. They totally did not understand him. They restrained his freedom, violated his privacy, and hated his friends. They also refused to give him two hundred and fifty dollars for a rock concert.

"Do you see any solution?" Giovanni asked the boy.

"None. We have nothing in common—nothing!"

"Why?"

"Maybe it's because . . . they are very old."

"How old are they?"

"My mother is thirty-eight. My father is forty-two. Believe me, I would love them, honest to God, if they were younger. About my age, for instance, or, maybe, two or three years older."

There seems to be only a thin line between tears of grief and tears of joy. The boo-hoos became ha-has. Ushers came around offering tissues. Some criers felt quite offended because of the sudden hilarity.

The third speaker was obese and shabby, with a frost of dandruff flakes on his round shoulders. He said that he was "lucky" because his parents were both dead. His problem was with his wife. He loved her but had never learned how to show it. He shyly confessed that his sex life with her was nil and that he subscribed to a dozen porn magazines for his own pleasure.

"What a schmuck!" Brenda snapped out of the corner of her mouth. "Instead of spending the five hundred bucks to come here, he would have done better buying a bottle of Head and Shoulders, a new shirt, and some flowers for his wife."

"I have a suggestion for you, sir," said Giovanni. "Get a copy of the *Kama Sutra* and read it together with your wife. Then, one day, approach you wife when she is sitting in a comfortable chair. Hug her, kiss her, and tell her what is in your heart. Nobody on earth can understand you better . . ."

That night, we played yet another game, Touching and Groping. Again the lights were dimmed, and we were all on our knees, choosing a partner. The passive ones were supposed to close their eyes and be perfectly still and quiet. The active ones were to initiate physical contact by using the "Braille" system. With their fingertips, they were to trace the forehead, eyes, cheeks, lips, nose, and neck of their partners. The rest of the body was off limits.

I happened to like this game very much. My partner was a handsome young man with long, tender fingers. I enjoyed a few wonderful passive moments and wouldn't mind finding out his phone number. I was most surprised to learn, however, that my new American compatriots hated this game. Later, at the discussion, they admitted to being made extremely uncomfortable by the touch of a stranger. If they had lived in the Soviet Union, where one is not touched but rather squished daily by strangers on public transportation and in those endless food and clothing queues, they would have been used to it. If they lived in a communal apartment and shared the kitchen and the only bathroom with seven unrelated people, they wouldn't be so afraid of the human touch. To me, it was sweet nostalgia.

In direct contrast to the quiet Touching and Groping game, the next exercise was wild and noisy. Partner *A* had one minute to tell partner *B* about his secret dream. Partner *B* also had one minute to prove to partner *A* that his dream was stupid, that he was a dumb jerk with no willpower. Partner

A then had to defend himself using his intelligence, experience, and personal conviction that his dream would indeed come true.

The ballroom turned into a Mid Eastern bazaar. People yelled and gesticulated wildly. Tempers flared. Charlie Green was paired with Brenda, and she was the first to speak.

"I want to be on stage in the limelight. I want to be like Diane Sawyer or Oprah Winfrey. I love fame. I have been dreaming about it all my life."

But good Charlie Green got ecstatic. "That's great! How wonderful! You really have what it takes. You could even be like Barbara Walters."

This couple got so carried away that they were unaware of the presence of Mr. Denino.

"Wrong! All wrong! Charlie, you are not supposed to encourage her. You are supposed to tell her that she cannot succeed and that all her dreams are foolish."

"Don't be silly. I think she's terrific. She'll make it." Charlie was hopeless.

I told my partner my dream, "I want to make a pile of money in real estate and become a capitalist barracuda."

My partner obeyed the rules: "No way, you never will. Listen to your accent. Your English sucks. Besides, you're reserved and shy, and you just don't have what it takes."

I was shocked by the sincerity in his voice. "Oh, you're right. It was just a stupid dream." It was the first time during the entire seminar when I cried.

At the beginning of the Realization seminar, we were promised that we would be reborn. As we all know, one has to die in order to be born again, so our last exercise was to be—Death! All the participants formed groups of nine. Once again the lights were dimmed and sad music was turned on. One person in each group lay on the floor, pretending to be dead. The other eight participants, four on each side, bent over the "corpse" with palms spread under the "body," conveying warm vibrations to the "deceased." Slowly and tenderly the "mourners" lifted the "body" off the floor to shoulder height and began to rock it rhythmically. When it was my turn to be the stiff, I was scared that they would drop me from the cat's cradle. I was sorry that I hadn't lost twenty pounds when I planned to. Finally, they lowered me to the floor, stood me up, and then did a group hug and kiss welcoming the "new" me back to the "new" world.

According to Mr. Denino, during those four days at Howard Johnson's we were supposed to leave behind our old baggage, such as low self-esteem, fears, and weaknesses. Our new baggage, which we were supposed to take home, included our new strengths, high self-esteem, new peace-making tools, and new knowledge of how to listen, how to speak, how to love, and how to make money. Have we succeeded? I cannot speak for everyone, but I learned only that "things are what they are."

I had been suffering terrible insomnia all through the seminar and needed to catch up on my sleep in the worst way. My digestive system was rebelling, and I wondered if I was permanently addicted to the *Rocky* trumpets. My emotional fuses were very short. I had completely forgotten about my original plan not to get emotionally involved.

Brenda's blood pressure was at an all-time high. Some folks broke out in hives. Calamine lotion was passed around in the rest rooms, and aspirin was secretly gobbled up like candy. Our arms and legs became numb, and an epidemic of hiccups was spreading fast.

"Do you think we have already reached hell, or are we still in purgatory?" I asked Brenda on the last morning.

She shrugged her shoulders. "I'm falling apart. That damn sculptor! He twisted my limbs out of joint."

We called a taxi and left the marble hall of Howard Johnson's behind. The day was sunny and glorious. The Charles River spread before us like glistening brocade.

"You look like a dead octopus yourself," Brenda said in the cab going home. "Do you need a few days off?"

"Oh no. Tomorrow morning I'll be in the office bright and early. I think I miss my real estate."

The cab driver perked up, "Are you ladies in real estate? Let me ask you . . ."

By the time our born-again team—that is, Brenda and I—got home, we had a listing for the taxi driver's condo and a request to find him a two-family house.

Epilogue: Years Later

Many years ago, back in Leningrad, while walking along Nevsky Prospekt, the main avenue of my beloved city, I noticed a new technological development—a moving electronic advertisement on the roof of the Aurora cinema. It said, "Starting tomorrow the third part of the epic movie *War and Peace* will be shown at the theaters near you. Finally you will be able to learn the fate of your favorite heroes."

This advertisement became the butt of many jokes in Leningrad because *War and Peace* is part of the Russian literature curriculum in all high schools and there is no need to see any movie to find out the fate of its heroes.

However, this flashback seems to be rather appropriate for the end of this book.

Recently our family celebrated its fifteenth anniversary of leaving Russia. Since then my husband, Tolya Dargis, has become a professor of computer science at Boston University. Our daughter, Katya, graduated from Barnard College and got her Ph.D. in economics at Yale. She is now working as a senior research fellow at the Federal Reserve Bank in Boston. From the windows of her office one can see the Atlantic Ocean. During her years at Yale, she met Michael, also an immigrant from Leningrad, who was a student of the Yale Medical School. They got married and produced two children, Daniel and Vicki, my dearest people on this planet. We all speak Russian at home, but the minute the kids are left alone they switch to their native English.

My mother got used to living in the Western hemisphere and published a book of poems and a collection of short stories, *For as Long as We Are Remembered* (in Russian).

As for me, I did not become a good real estate broker despite the Realization seminar. The essence of the broker's profession is to sell. But it turned out that I hate to sell and love to buy. Besides, I was too emotional about it and considered every aborted sale a personal failure and the end of the world. So, after a few years I quit my job as a real estate broker.

For as long as I can remember, I had wanted to be a writer. It looks now like my dream has finally come true. I have published three books in Russian, and one of them has even been translated into English, Italian, and Hungarian. For the last three years, I've been working as a journalist at the Russian-American Broadcasting Corporation. My weekly talk show is called *On the Road Again*.

For years I was nostalgic for my misty Leningrad. This nostalgia tormented me till the day I decided to go back for a visit. The Soviet Union had ceased to exist; my beloved Leningrad had become St. Petersburg. I wandered through the streets where I lived and went to school. I sat on the bench in the Aleksandrovsky Park where I was kissed for the first time in my life. Finally, I dared to go into the apartment building I used to call home.

Standing in front of the entrance, I could feel my heart beat. I climbed to the second floor. Shreds of blackened insulation and charred felt still stuck out from the door to our former apartment . . .

"Thank God, I don't live here anymore," I thought, sighing with relief. I have never looked back again.

About the Author

The author of this book is a female of many ambiguities. She is a person of uncertain age: somewhere between forty and sixty, depending on lighting. She has many professions: a woman of letters by calling, a geologist by training, a real estate broker by necessity, and a housewife, if everything else fails. Her nationality is also uncertain: in the former Soviet Union she was considered Jewish; in the United States, Russian; in Israel, American. She lives in Boston, loves New York, and longs for misty St. Petersburg. Her favorite season is autumn; her favorite weather, light rain; her favorite time of day, dusk. At dusk, according to an old Russian proverb, all ladies look beautiful, and all cats look gray . . . And gray is her favorite color.